A CENTER IN THE CYCLONE

Twenty-First Century Clergy Self-Care

Bruce Epperly

An Alban Institute Book

ROWMAN & LITTLEFIELD
Lanham • Boulder • New York • London

Published by Rowman & Littlefield
A wholly owned subsidiary of The Rowman & Littlefield Publishing Group,
Inc.
4501 Forbes Boulevard, Suite 200, Lanham, Maryland 20706
www.rowman.com

16 Carlisle Street, London W1D 3BT, United Kingdom

British Library Cataloguing in Publication Information Available

Library of Congress Cataloging-in-Publication Data

Epperly, Bruce Gordon.
A center in the cyclone : twenty-first century clergy self-care / Bruce Epperly.
pages cm
Includes bibliographical references.
ISBN 978-1-56699-757-7 (cloth : alk. paper) — ISBN 978-1-56699-713-3 (pbk. : alk. paper) —
ISBN 978-1-56699-714-0
1. Pastoral theology. I. Title.
BV4014.E67 2014
248.8'92—dc23
2014016459

∞™ The paper used in this publication meets the minimum requirements of
American National Standard for Information Sciences Permanence of Paper
for Printed Library Materials, ANSI/NISO Z39.48-1992.

Printed in the United States of America

CONTENTS

WORDS OF THANKS

I am confident of this, that the one who began a good work among you will bring it to completion by the day of Jesus Christ . . . having produced the harvest of righteousness that comes through Jesus Christ for the glory and praise of God.

—Philippians 1:6, 11

God is doing a good work in our lives and in the world. God is doing a good work in the lives of pastors and congregations. All good works, like the good seed of Jesus's parable of the sower and the seed, need to be nurtured so that they will bear good and healthy fruit. This vision of hopeful ministry is the inspiration for my commitment to clergy well-being, wholeness, and excellence and for my calling as pastor of South Congregational Church, United Church of Christ, in Centerville, Massachusetts.

This text is written in the context of hundreds of conversations I've had with pastors over the past decade. Many of them confess that the cares of ministry in the twenty-first century have nearly choked the life out of their ministry. Many pastors are overwhelmed by the perfect storm of too many responsibilities, too few resources, and too rapid congregational, cultural, and technological changes. We are in a time of great spiritual awakening among Christians, people of other faiths, and self-described spiritual but not religious seekers. Insightful spiritual leadership is needed now more than ever to navigate the waves of pluralism, postmodernism, and globalism. Spiritual leaders need to sharpen their mission, administration, outreach, and preaching skills, but they also need to deepen their commitments to spiritual growth and self-care practices to insure healthy and effective ministry over the long haul.

As I corresponded with pastors in North America and, occasionally, by Facebook in Great Britain, I realized that I had at least twelve texts hidden within the twelve chapters of this book. I also recognized that I needed to be both humble and bold in reflecting on pathways to healthy ministry and pastoral self-care. While I couldn't say everything in one book, I could paint a theological, spiritual, and narrative portrait of healthy ministry in the twenty-first century. My goal was to dialogue with Roy Oswald's groundbreaking book *Clergy Self-Care* in light of the unique spiritual, theological, cultural, and technological context of the second decade of the twenty-first century. I am grateful to Roy Oswald's insights in 1991 and their ongoing value to pastors today. My goal is to provide a resource for holistic personal and professional transformation and healing for pastors in the second decade of the twenty-first century. As pastors experience greater wholeness, they will be more equipped to be effective spiritual leaders, proclaiming God's vision of shalom for the long haul of professional ministry.

It has taken a village of pastors to inspire the writing of this book. Some I have known for decades; others I have recently met on Facebook or at lectures, clergy groups, and retreats. I am grateful for their commitment and willingness to share their challenges, dreams, and practices. I am grateful to Richard Bass, editorial director at Alban Institute, for his affirmation of the need for a twenty-first-century text on clergy self-care and to my editor, Fritz Gutwein, for his encouragement, support, and care for the quality of this text. I gathered a group of diverse pastors and spiritual leaders to read the text. I wanted to address diversities in age, gender, marital status, experience, and denominational affiliation. This book is richer as a result of their insights. I give a special word of thanks to Tiffany Bidwell, Bob Cornwall, Patricia Adams Farmer, Ruth Harvey, Ricky Phillips, Anna Rollins, and Cyndi Simpson for their comments on the text. These working pastors reminded me of omissions and encouraged me to be inclusive in responding to issues relating to pastors in each season of ministry. I am grateful to Kate Epperly, whose companionship and love are always a source of inspiration as we share our journey of ministry, grandparenting, and domestic life. Finally, I dedicate this book to the memory of my parents, Everett Lewis Epperly and Loretta Victoria Epperly, from whom I learned both the joys and the challenges of ministry, and to my first ministerial mentor John Akers, whose support enabled me to see myself initially as a scholar and later as a pastor. I also dedicate this text to the faithful community at South Congregational Church in Centerville on Cape Cod, where I look forward to many years of vital, transformative, and healthy ministry. God's good work led to a harvest of righteousness in their lives that they have conveyed to me. May this same blessing fill your life and ministry.

MINISTRY IN THE TWENTY-FIRST CENTURY

God is our refuge and strength,
    a very present help in trouble.
Therefore we will not fear, though the earth should change,
    though the mountains shake in the heart of the sea;
though its waters roar and foam,
    though the mountains tremble with its tumult.
There is a river whose streams make glad the city of God,
    the holy habitation of the Most High.
God is in the midst of the city; it shall not be moved;
    God will help it when the morning dawns.
The nations are in an uproar, the kingdoms totter;
    he utters his voice, the earth melts.
The LORD of hosts is with us;
    the God of Jacob is our refuge. . . .
"Be still, and know that I am God!
    I am exalted among the nations,
    I am exalted in the earth."
The LORD of hosts is with us;
    the God of Jacob is our refuge.

—Psalm 46:1–7, 10–11

FROM URGENCY TO CALM

"**W**hy did I ever make social media a part of my ministry? I wanted to respond to the youth and young adults in our church and to the spiritual but not religious folk in the community, but this is getting ridiculous. I'm spending more time online than on face-to-face pastoral ministry," Doug complained to his wife as he awakened Friday morning—his day off—to one hundred responses to a Twitter comment he made the night before. In addition to that, his professional e-mail account contained twenty new messages, most relating to the upcoming Christmas Eve worship services. He knew that any response he made on Twitter or Facebook would inspire twenty responses in return. As he imagined his morning slipping away from him, this forty-eight-year-old, high-functioning United Methodist pastor felt caught between a rock and a hard place. "If I don't respond to their queries today, some of the worship team members will become anxious and think something's wrong, but even a short comment on Twitter or the church's group mail will initiate another avalanche of responses. And then what will I do? Just responding to their angst will be more work for me. I wish I didn't know half of what's going on in this church! It's only eight o'clock, and I feel like my day off is slipping away from me. Help!" Doug cried. After an hour and a half of e-mail communication, Doug finally allowed himself to take a long run and begin his abbreviated day off, a matinee and supper with his wife, Sandra, a United Methodist pastor in a neighboring town. But, as usual, she joined the chorus of pastoral lamentation on the ride to the theater. "I love the new media and the possibilities it brings to my ministry. It's exciting to have an online discussion about a YouTube video, a group reflecting on Twitter about Downton Abbey, or a Facebook discussion about a provocative film, but it seems like most of my ministry is done in front of the computer. I miss the good old days—just a few years back—when I could do most of my ministerial contacts at a local coffeehouse."[1]

Later that weekend, when Doug shared his experience with his father, a retired United Methodist pastor, his father was amazed at the changes that had occurred in the ten years since he served his last congregation. "I guess I quit in the nick of time, son," he confessed. "I started using e-mail in the late 1980s, but even then we used it only for special events. There was no such thing as Group-Mail, Google, text messaging, or Facebook. I didn't have an iPhone or text messaging or even a cell phone. When I was home, folks called me on the phone and I could screen calls with my answering machine. When I was on pastoral calls, I simply let my secretary know I would be at the hospital or visiting a particular family and would be unavailable for the afternoon. Emergencies just had to wait till I got the message. Now, everything seems so urgent, and pastors are too busy to do the person-to-person ministry that was the heart of my work. In the old days, my time was my own. I can't imagine doing ministry with so many interruptions and so-called emergencies. You have my prayers, son!"

Sally loves to read. A Lutheran (ELCA) pastor, she gets her best ideas at the local coffee shop with a latte in one hand and a book in the other. Over a coffee at a DC coffeehouse, Sally noted that, "Just for fun, I read the Mitford series by Jan Karon. These are great books and fun to read, and they give some insights into ministry. But, they're about as real as reality TV! No pastor works that way today! Still, some days I wish my ministry was more like Father Tim's—making house calls, spending an hour each morning at the local café, accidently running into people on the street, and taking leisurely walks around town as a way of encountering congregants. But then I say to myself, 'Let's get real' as I face fifty unanswered e-mails and seven text messages in the last hour and two cell-phone conversations. Father Tim could hide out, but my congregants can get ahold of me twenty-four/seven. Sometimes I receive text messages at midnight with the introductory greeting, 'I don't want to disturb your family, but this is important, so I texted you. You can respond when you get up.' Don't these [expletive deleted] people ever sleep? What's so [expletive deleted] important here at church that they can't wait till tomorrow. Father Tim could revolt against using e-mail, but if I took a week off from answering messages, there would be calls for my resignation!"

Over the past decade, I've heard comments like these, each with its own nuance and emotional temperature, hundreds of times in my work with clergy in every season and locale of ministry. Many of today's clergy feel like they are on duty twenty-four/seven. They and their congregants have a profound sense of urgency. Time and money are scarce and anxiety is in the air. Everything is important and everything needs to be addressed right now, or better yet, yesterday. But, as one pastor noted, following his decision to leave his cell phone on the shelf to go on a walk with his partner, leaving his administrative assistant in charge of his calls for a few hours: "Is everything really that urgent? Most things can wait for a few hours, if not a few days!"

Twenty years ago Roy Oswald wrote his classic on clergy stress and well-being, *Clergy Self-Care*.[2] Oswald's words on stress, burnout, and family alienation still ring true to the experiences of many pastors. But one thing has changed: the proliferation of external stimuli and the resulting bondage many pastors feel to devices initially intended to save labor and enhance communication with their congregants and potential new members. Today's pastors must intentionally seek a peaceful center in the cyclone of ministerial challenges to experience wholeness, joy, inspiration, and excellence in ministry. Change theorist Peter Vaill once described institutional life in terms of "constant whitewater," and this constant whitewater applies to congregational and denominational life today. But as Psalm 46 asserts, even in the rapids, with roaring waters all around, an adept navigator can experience spiritual centeredness. In the midst of a maelstrom of demands, spiritual-centered pastors can "be still, " and know that God is with us. Even in the storm, Jesus was able to rest in the back of the boat, trusting God's providential care but prepared to be ready when his followers needed him.

PASTORS AS PROFESSIONAL GENERALISTS

Along with family medical practitioners, congregational pastors are among the last professional generalists. Pastors—and especially solo pastors—are asked to perform a variety of tasks, for which they had in many cases received virtually no training in seminary or field education. Recently I asked a group of pastors to describe the tasks they perform in a usual day. Hands shot up and they responded:

Check and respond to e-mail.
Write a blog for the church website.
Put out relational fires among laypeople and staff.
Study for sermons.
Write articles for the electronic or print church newsletter or both.
Manage employees and volunteers.
Prepare for Bible studies, confirmation and baptismal classes, and
    lay education programs.

Attend denominational meetings.

Inspect the building for cleanliness and safety and insure there's
   toilet paper and paper towels in the rest rooms.

Work with contractors and repair people.

Make hospital visits.

Make home visits and deliver communion.

Conduct funerals and provide grief counseling.

Respond to natural disasters or community tragedies.

Place ads in the newspaper and notices on the website.

Recruit Sunday school teachers and committee members.

Convene and participate in congregational meetings.

Mediate disputes related to the nursery school or other organiza-
   tions that use the building.

Check financial reports and spreadsheets.

Unplug toilets and mop floors.

Provide spiritual direction with congregants.

Lead congregational visioning and strategic planning sessions.

Participate in the local ministerium or interfaith groups.

Sit on local, regional, and national denominational committees.

Meet with congregational leaders.

Help families respond to the needs of elderly parents.

Care for my own spiritual and intellectual life.

Update the church's website.

Respond to issues of social concern in the community.

Meet with potential members.

Plan worship and work with the church musician(s).

Keep up with current events.

Read articles and books related to ministry, spirituality, theology,
   and leadership.

Even though I had been a minister for more than thirty years, by the
time this group of skilled and committed pastors enumerated their
many tasks of ministry, I was ready to take a nap. Moreover, a minister's
day follows no typical schedule. I recall being in the middle of preparing a sermon when I took a break to cross the street from the pastor's
study to do some copying in the church office. Something must have
lured me to the lower level where a Lenten potluck dinner was to be
held later that day. To my chagrin, I discovered the previous night's rain
had flooded the social hall. I promptly called the property chair and

always work to do.

then began mopping the floor. An hour later, when the property chair and his brother-in-law finally arrived to help out, I was still mopping and had forgotten many of the ideas I had hoped to include in my message. When I experienced the call to ministry, I never imagined that it would involve custodial work along with preaching, teaching, and pastoral care.

Although other professionals may make themselves available "after hours," most attorneys, physicians, and therapists have set hours and don't expect to encounter patients seeking their counsel or making complaints at the local supermarket, at a movie, or on a family excursion. Congregants often preface their intrusions with "I know you're busy" or "I don't want to bother you on your night off," but then they plunge into an issue about a difficult child, something they saw on television related to the life of Jesus, or a controversial social issue. There isn't much "Miller Time" for ministers unless they are intentional about how they balance ministry, personal life, study, and relationships. As one minister noted, "This is a wonderful profession. I love being part of people's lives and sharing the good news of salvation. I'm never sure what's going to happen next. No two days are ever alike and every day brings surprises. Still, there are days when the pain and joy of human life is almost too much to bear. Those days, I need to retreat, if only for a few minutes, to experience the challenges of ministry as joyful interruptions and not time-consuming or energy-depleting nuisances." Another minister added, "I love this work. It's never boring or routine. But some days, as the commercial says, 'life comes at you fast' and I have to get out of the way so I won't get hit by the debris! Just this past week, I had two unexpected deaths and a local tragedy, and I had to respond to these while planning and leading the Holy Week services."

Given their vocation as ministerial generalists, congregants expect the pastor to know something about everything and respond to crises great and small, often at the drop of a hat. This can be a source of excitement and humor as well as frustration. I recall a humorous coffee hour incident during my tenure as interim pastor of a midsized United Church of Christ town and country congregation in Central Maryland. Happily enjoying a Krispy Kreme donut and a cup of coffee, I was confronted by a matriarch of the church. Knowing that I was also a seminary professor, she had a burning question and needed an immediate response: "Last night I was watching a program on biblical miracles on the Discovery Channel and they talked about the sun standing still at Jericho. How did that happen, Pastor Bruce?" I about choked. Despite a PhD in theology, I was unprepared for her question. "Damn the Discovery Channel!" I said to myself. "And why right now? I'm just trying to get a break after worship." I knew that the question was important to her, and I also knew that it was a theological minefield involving the nuances of biblical interpretation, the meaning of miracles, and the authority of Scripture. In retrospect, I'm sure I did not give her a satisfactory answer, but for the moment she seemed content that her PhD pastor took her question seriously. Five minutes later I found myself sitting around a church school table with a handful of twelve-year-olds, exploring with them what it means to follow Jesus in middle school. All in a pastor's day! It's a great life, but it can wear you down.

THE ADVENTURES OF TWENTY-FIRST CENTURY PASTORS

I believe that ministry is always concrete, contextual, and current. While we may sing about the "old, old story" and affirm the great traditions of the church in worship and theology, most pastors know that good ministry is always done in the present tense. I still recall the critique given of a pastor who chose to preach on the Sunday after September 11, 2001, as if nothing cataclysmic had occurred. I recently felt dissatisfied when in the course of worship, the pastor made only a passing reference to the massacre of children at the Sandy Hook Elementary School. His sermon and worship leadership were adequate, but the omission left me wondering if he really connected with the congregants that day, many of whom were parents of elementary school children. There are tried and true habits of effective spiritual leaders, but pastoral practices are always embodied in space and time. Excellent, effective, and spiritually centered pastors share a commitment to prayer, study, continuing education, psychological maturity, self-reflection, compassionate listening, visionary thinking, and justice seeking, but living out these qualities of good ministry varies depending on the context and circumstances of ministry. I am sure that the leisurely approach of Father Tim in Jan Karon's novels was adequate for a pastor-centered, small-town, family church in the 1950s; I am equally certain that Father Tim might not be as successful in a multicultural urban setting or even in many of today's rural congregations, whose congregants may work locally but think globally as a result of the World Wide Web. As a walker, I am attracted to the idea of pastoring on foot, but peripatetic ministry takes place only in small towns and densely populated neighborhoods; in truth, most of my urban and countryside ministry has joined the quiet of contemplation and study with the hustle and bustle of commuting by car from one call or meeting to the next.

I admire the portrait of a pastor's vocation portrayed in the movie *A River Runs through It*. Faithful to his calling as a Presbyterian minister, Revered Maclean pores over the Scriptures and the classics of Western literature in search of the right word or turn of phrase. His book-lined study is a monument to scholarship. On days off, he and his sons journey to the Blackfoot River, near Missoula, Montana, for mornings of quiet fly fishing. As an introverted scholar, I love this image of the pastoral life and try to emulate it whenever possible. However, my experience is that ministry has often been more about managing limited resources, reconciling factions, balancing budgets, recruiting volunteers, nurturing and guiding staff members than about hours of scholarship and sermon preparation. Ministry is an adventure, now more than ever, and today's pastors need creative ways to join high tech with high touch for the healing of people and institutions.

TEN CHALLENGES FOR TWENTY-FIRST CENTURY PASTORS

In reflecting on the current external and internal challenges and stressors of ministry, I consulted the one reference no pastor can do without today—Facebook. I asked my Facebook friends, many of whom are currently involved in the ministry, to consider "how ministry has changed in the past twenty years" since Roy Oswald's groundbreaking book, and "how, if you are new to ministry, senior colleagues describe these changes." Their responses were not exhaustive, although they clearly reflected the challenges these high-functioning, effective, and committed pastors face doing ministry in the twenty-first century. Ministry has always been challenging, but pastors can, with the author of the epistle of James, "Experience nothing but joy" (James 1:2) if they respond to God's movements of grace and healing within the ordinary as well as dramatic responsibilities of effective and excellent ministry.")

In the course of my personal and Facebook conversations, I was able to identify ten challenges that most pastors face in the first decades of the twenty-first century. I suspect these are just the tip of the iceberg for full-time and bivocational pastors today.

Challenge 1: Technology, Accessibility, and Social Media

Every Sunday night in the 1950s and early '60s, our family ate popcorn and apples while watching Walter Cronkite's *Twentieth Century*, which later morphed into *The Twenty-First Century* and eventually *60 Minutes*. I recall the sagely Cronkite, America's most trusted media figure at the time, noting that in the twenty-first century, people will need to find new ways to deal with their leisure time; they'll simply have so much of it! Just tell that to a twenty-first century pastor, embedded within the rapidly moving world of social media. Whether by choice or necessity many pastors, like their business counterparts, are constantly checking their e-mail on their iPhones or smartphones, looking up information on Google or Bing while speaking with a colleague, spouse, or child, and consulting the ever-increasing volume of voice mails and text messages. The proliferation of communication technologies has virtually eliminated the boundary between work time and off time. After all, it takes no effort to check your e-mail if your phone is always with you. "One look won't hurt or get in the way of time with my child, friend, partner, spouse, will it?" we say to ourselves. When that minute morphs into half an hour and our companion becomes impatient, we often react with "It will be just a minute more. I'm almost done," despite the fact that this is our sabbath or our day off. "If I don't watch out, I'm on duty all the time," a midcareer Unitarian Universalist pastor confessed. A United Church of Christ interim pastor I know noted his office hours in the church newsletter and then added, as if to apologize for not being in the office every day of the week, "You can reach me twenty-four/seven on my cell phone." I wondered, as I pondered his gracious invitation, whether he really meant what he said. Does he really welcome calls at three in the morning? Is it good for this pastor to have no apparent boundary between work and home? Does his availability diminish the quality of time with his family or in prayer and study? Does our quest for one more medium to promote professional excellence ultimately threaten our ability to embody professional and personal excellence in the concrete realities of our family, our spiritual practices, and our pastoral leadership?

These are issues most pastors, even in rural areas, face today. They can be boiled down to a question a Disciples of Christ pastor asked me at a "Tending to the Holy" workshop at Lake Junaluska Conference Center in North Carolina: "How can I use my technology in ways that help simplify my life and improve my ministry rather than becoming the servant of the technology that's meant to make my life easier?" I resonate with his concerns as I seek to join high-touch with high-tech ministry in my new pastorate in one of Cape Cod's villages.

Moreover, the use of current technologies raises a variety of relational and ethical issues. Virtually every pastor has found her- or himself caught in the middle of electronic communications that lack the nuance of face-to-face conversations. I personally find critiques on e-mail much more intense and alienating than the give and take of a lively face-to-face conversation. Many people feel that they have permission to blow off steam on e-mail that they would be too courteous or timid to share in person. But once written, and often these "honest" communications come from pastors about congregants or congregational situations, such caustic comments can't be taken back and may lead to more "honest" and unhelpful electronic interchanges from those whom they have just scolded. Sadly, many pastors and congregants fail to take the sagely advice of singer-songwriter Carrie Newcomer's song "Don't Press Send."

Despite its value for communication and information sharing, not to mention congregational outreach and mission, social media and Internet accessibility blurs the lines between private and public and confidential and open communication. A pastor recently admitted the challenges of using Facebook: "Who should I 'friend' on Facebook? If a congregant requests to be a Facebook friend, should I 'accept'? What type of communication is appropriate on Facebook? Do I need two accounts, one for church and one for personal use?" She then admitted that "two accounts is just too complicated. I'll just have to be mindful of every comment I make." I advised one pastor to prune her Facebook comments after I read the following: "I really got trashed last night." I counseled another pastor to be more circumspect when he aired his feelings about his lay leaders on Facebook or made a disparaging comment about people who viewed Fox News.

While technological changes have complicated ministry, they have also enabled pastors to be more effective in ministry, especially with young adults. A midtwenties United Methodist pastor, whose focus is Christian Education and Youth ministry, averred, "I don't view technology as a burden or overload . . . it comes naturally." She added an illuminating comment that many older pastors need to heed: "I think when young people communicate with other young people via text or e-mail instead of face to face, they view the conversation just as seriously and don't necessarily need a follow-up in person. If it weren't for texting, I think some of my youth would not talk with me at all. I often use texting for pastoral care. It may lack the nuance, but that's how I reach people my age and younger." But, as a caveat, she noted that "young clergy do need to realize that older generations don't necessarily feel the same way. Some may feel left out if they don't have an e-mail account, and most church business is communicated electronically."

Challenge 2: Time

How often have you heard a pastor admit the following: "With all that I have to do at church, I barely have time to study anymore . . . spend time with my family . . . exercise . . . prepare my sermons"? A Central Pennsylvania Mennonite pastor recently confided in me: "I feel like I'm chasing my tail. I never really stop and on my days off or with my family, I still think about work. There is so much pain and so much to do for God's kingdom. I go to sleep tired and wake up tired every morning."

Our accessibility is closely connected to our experience of time. Do we have enough time to balance the tasks of ministry, relationships, and self-care? Are we always on the go, never stopping to reflect on the quality of our interactions and job performance? Do we have too much on our plate, not just every day but every week? Do we work regularly more than fifty hours a week? How you respond to these questions will radically shape your ministry and may be a matter of personal and professional well-being or dis-ease.

Every parent and pastor knows that we cannot manage time or control the events of our lives. A phone call announcing the death of a congregation's matriarch can turn a pastor's week upside down. Calls need to be made, family members visited, conversations initiated with funeral directors, former pastors, and lay participants, not to mention preparing the homily and worship service and consulting with the church musician. A natural catastrophe, such as a snowstorm, tornado, earthquake, or hurricane, or a community tragedy, such as a bus accident or a massacre at a local school or theater, means all hands on deck and long hours spent consoling the victims and their families, often for weeks, along with insuring that the work of the church continues with grace and excellence. Everything has to be dropped to be a good pastor in times of crisis. Yet pastors do not need to be at the mercy of unexpected events.

Scripture says, ("Where there is no vision, the people perish" (Prov. 29:18, King James Version). The same applies to pastors: without a vision, the pastor perishes and is at the mercy of others' agendas, expectations, and schedules) We can't control time, but we can be intentional about our attitudes toward time and the expected and unexpected events of pastoral ministry. (Intentionality is essential to self-care and effective ministry.) Intentionality, grounded in an inspirational vision of ministry and personal life, enables us to navigate the permanent white water of ministry and it provides a context within which we can distinguish between the urgent, important, and optional demands of ministry.

Physician Larry Dossey notes the dangerous impact of what he calls "hurry sickness" or "time sickness" on our overall spiritual, emotional, and physical health. Our attitudes toward time can be a source of either wellness or stress. The best antidote for time sickness involves living by a spiritual-theological vision that enables us to let go of the inessential and free ourselves from other people's "emergencies," while intentionally committing ourselves to being fully present in the many active and contemplative tasks of ministry.

Challenge 3: Authority and Expectations

Among the Reformed-United Church of Christ churches of Central Pennsylvania, many newly ordained pastors invoke the term Herr Pastor or Herr Doktor Pastor to describe how congregants felt about their pastors in the "good old days" of the congregations established by German immigrants. Pastors were typically among the most educated people in their communities. They commanded respect both in the pulpit and in the community. Their word was law in congregational life; it was assumed the "pastor knows best." While most of these newly ordained pastors seek to embody a more egalitarian approach to ministry, grounded in their commitment to equipping the laity to take responsibility for the life of the church, some pastors wish that their position commanded more implicit authority among congregants. A veteran United Church of Christ pastor shared his misgivings about the current state of ministry: "Pastors today find themselves in a perfect storm of professional challenges. They have much less authority among their congregants than pastors of previous generations. At the same time, congregants have greater expectations of their ministers in terms of effectiveness, flexibility, and competence. My colleagues and I often feel like we're between a rock and a hard place. We have more demands and greater expectations from our congregants and fewer resources to do the task of ministry." Another United Church of Christ pastor chimed in, "We can't be expert at everything, nor can we be held fully accountable for congregational growth or decline. The pastor can't do it alone; he or she needs committed partners among her or his congregants to succeed in ministry."

Challenge 4: Changing Shape of Lay Involvement and Participation

Pastors and congregations are experiencing increased stress as a result of changing demographics, especially the aging of the boomer and builder generations, and new shapes of lay involvement and participation. Congregations often expect to maintain the same programs as they did in the 1950s and '60s, despite the fact that many of these programs were initiated at a time when most women were stay-at-home moms and implicit blue laws—as well as good taste—made Sunday mornings off-limits for children's sporting events, professional athletic games, mercantile activities, and movies. Today, the church is just one of many possibilities for families on Sunday mornings. Soccer and baseball practices and swim meets and dance contests often trump church attendance in the eyes of parents who see athletics as the pathway to good health and success for their children. One pastor complained, "These days I can barely put together a youth group or confirmation class. The children are so booked that even weekday Christian formation classes are eclipsed by music lessons, computer classes, and sports practice. When I was young, all the kids went to summer church camp and attended Sunday night youth group. But not today! These parents want their children to grow as Christians but place church involvement below sports camp, soccer, and swimming lessons when push comes to shove. Church camps barely rate because of their limited Internet access. I can't shame them into sending their children to confirmation class or Sunday school, or tell them that it's unlikely their children will perform like David Beckham, Kobe Bryant, or Serena Williams. But they judge my work based on their children's participation. I'm not a pied piper. It's a no-win situation for pastors today."

Pastors also struggle to involve adults in the life of the church. Tasks that in previous eras had routinely been done by laypeople either are left undone or default to the pastor. The changing face of professionalism has made it virtually impossible to hold women's groups during the day or to rouse the hospitality committee to cater a funeral. With the passing of the greatest generation and the older baby boomers, this situation will only get more challenging as it affects lay leadership and financial support.

Challenge 5: Boundary Issues

Pastoral ministry is a sacred task. We are the children of the shaman, prophets, and healers. We are also representatives of God, called to shape our lives in accordance with the way of Jesus. Our role is to care for people, body, mind, and spirit, and this means that our primary relationships with congregants are mediated through our commitment to their spiritual care and well-being. When a pastor abuses her or his position sexually, financially, relationally, ideologically, or theologically, she places the spiritual lives of others at risk and damages Jesus's message of good news. Our character, lifestyle, and behavior are essential to healthy ministry, and we are called to maintain the highest standards of conduct in every aspect of our lives, most especially in our vocation as pastors.

Still, as essential as boundary keeping is to ministry, pastoral understandings of professional norms and boundaries can be a source of significant relational and personal stress. Three comments by high-functioning and ethically conscious ministers reflect the stresses that current emphases on appropriate boundaries place on pastors. As a small-town, single, Lutheran pastor, Sharon related her sense of guilt as she discovered that dual roles are unavoidable in rural and small town ministries. "I worry that I'm doing something wrong. All my friends live over an hour away. Sure, we talk regularly, but I can't just jump in the car to grab a cup of coffee or have dinner. My congregants really care for me, and so I end up eating with congregants two or three times a week. They bring over vegetables and pies and leftovers from their suppers. When my car broke down, I went to the local mechanic, and he's a church member and refuses to charge me for his labor. Recognizing that I receive a modest salary, a couple offered me their beach house for a week this summer. I need a vacation, and I know if I decline, they won't understand. They'll think I'm ungrateful. Still, I feel tension about the dual roles that are pervasive in my ministry. What am I supposed to do?"

An American Baptist pastor, Steve related the quandary he experienced when the chair of the board, with whom he'd had numerous coffee dates to discuss church business, revealed, "Steve, I'm glad we speak the same language and have developed a friendship. Your last two predecessors were cold fish. They were decent pastors, but I never really got to know them. I felt like they assumed we were two different breeds of animal—clergy and lay—and that put me off. I'm glad you're different." Steve was tempted to invoke the shibboleth employed by boundary training leaders and seminary professors: "I'm your pastor, not your friend." But he realized if he were that blunt, he would jeopardize the positive relationship he had with a key church member whose friendship had become important to him. "In articulating appropriate relational boundaries, I don't want to humiliate or alienate my parishioners by maintaining a legalistic by-the-book approach, but I also need the freedom to challenge as well as disappoint them with my approach to ministry."

Recently retired after fifteen years as pastor of a two-hundred-member county-seat church affiliated with the United Church of Christ, Marcia feels judged by her peers, disrespected by the current interim minister, and on notice by the judicatory staff. With anger in her voice, Marcia stated her concerns: "The minute I retired, I became an outcast. The powers that be think I'm going to be a nuisance in my former congregation. They tell me what I can and cannot do, as if I'm a small child or an accident waiting to happen. All this finger wagging really burns me up. I followed the rules and observed appropriate professional ethics. Now that I'm retired, they think I'm going to be a loose cannon. The interim had the audacity to tell me I shouldn't even attend the funeral of one of my dearest congregants, with whom I pastored during the final years of her life. It's as if all the relationships I've cultivated as a good pastor for so many years must be dumped the minute I leave. I know I'm in pain, and I also know this hurts congregants who want me to be there in their time of need."

The pain of leaving a beloved congregation is felt by clergy spouses as well as clergy. Helen, the spouse of an Episcopalian pastor, felt emotionally bereft when her husband retired after thirty years at the same parish. With tears in her eyes, she shared her grief: "When Daryl left the church, I had to leave it as well. For over thirty years, I spent every Thursday night in choir practices. My children grew up here and I became close to parents with children their age. Some of my happiest times were spent here at All Saints, and now I have to say good-bye forever."

Boundaries are challenging. Sadly, most boundary training focuses on the external behavior of the pastor rather than her or his character, emotions, maturity, and spiritual life. Pastoral differentiation involves the right blend of distance and intimacy; and without love for her or his congregants, a pastor will find it virtually impossible to be effective in ministry. Inflexible approaches to pastoral boundaries, legalistic and pathologically oriented in approach, hurt pastors and congregations alike. They create an implicit sense of guilt among pastors, even when they are doing what is necessary for healthy pastor-congregant relationships. Judicatories who eschew biblical fundamentalism often demand a type of professional inflexibility that adds stress to ministerial relationships. Still, as a result of the harm caused by former pastors who meddle in the life the church, criticize the current pastor, or try to maintain close pastoral relationships following their departure, former pastors need to be reminded that the well-being of the congregation and integrity of the ministerial profession trumps their personal needs.

Challenge 6: Finances

Virtually every pastor I speak with mentions the challenges of institutional and personal finances. Congregational finances are constantly in arrears, often subsidizing pastoral salaries and programs on a month-to-month basis from endowments and reserves. Some pastors who planned on full-time ministry have to put together two or three positions to honor their ministerial call. The perfect storm of demographics, the passing of the greatest generation, economic instability, lower interest rates on endowments and saving accounts, and rising health care and energy costs have led numerous congregations to consider reducing health and retirement benefits, freezing salaries, eliminating positions, and moving to part-time pastoral leadership. Almost every associate pastor I know lives with the reality that her or his position may be unfunded with next year's budget. As Debbie, an Ohio Presbyterian pastor, confessed, "I'm not sure where I'll be next year. It's hard to plan programs and imagine new initiatives when I know that my job may be eliminated in January. Last year, I escaped downsizing as a result of the generosity of one of the congregation's matriarchs who anted up $30,000 at the last minute. She can't do this every year. I love this church and my work with the youth and young adults, but I've just started circulating my ministerial profile. I want to jump before I'm pushed!"

A solo pastor of another Presbyterian church, following the departure of the associate pastor due to financial reasons, noted glumly, "Church membership hasn't declined nor have programs been eliminated. In fact, we have more members than five years ago, but also greater expenses. Now I will have to do the work of two pastors, since the laity hasn't picked up the slack in pastoral care. I may have to redefine my sense of ministry to survive here. Right now, I'm just swamped!"

A Disciples of Christ pastor living in a major metropolitan area, Oscar complained that he can barely get by on a salary that looks generous to many of his colleagues. "My wife had to quit her job for us to come to here. She's still looking, and meanwhile, my $90,000 combined salary and housing allowance barely pays the bills when entry-level homes in our area begin at $500,000. My friends from the country think I'm a fat cat, but my paycheck doesn't go far when $36,000 goes to housing and utilities. I just picked up two classes at the community college to help make ends meet."

Challenge 7: Globalism

John Wesley once noted that he looked upon the whole world as his parish. Wesley's affirmation is both a joyful reality and an oppressive burden for many pastors today. "My ministry is global these days," Mary averred. "To be faithful as a pastor I need to remind my congregants that they also are global citizens and that what happens in Sudan, Gaza, Syria, and Israel makes a difference in their lives. In my community, however, this means I have to keep up with my studies on international affairs as well as regularly attend denominational and ecumenical events focusing on hunger, human trafficking, refugees, and the environment. It's a part-time job just to keep up with what's going on locally and globally, especially when I have to be a leader in local justice issues as well."

Most pastors are committed to thinking globally and acting locally. They recognize that the gospel has global, economic, and political implications. They want to be partners in God's vision of shalom. Still, the quest to motivate and energize congregants to become globally and socially conscious citizens can consume a major portion of a pastor's work week. The demands of ministry become even more challenging when pastors commit themselves to directly helping to welcome and resettle refugee families, many of whom are political refugees. As one socially active Unitarian Universalist pastor acknowledges, "I wish there were more hours in the day. I can't ignore the suffering of the world. When I see something on television or the Internet, I need to respond and this church needs to respond. But how can I be a good pastor, husband, and parent with so many demands? My wife and children are not at risk from dictators or malnutrition, but sometimes I wonder if they are suffering because of my involvement in global affairs. The church's task is to change the world, but how do I care for the world right here, my wife and small children? I know that I'm not a good disciple; I can't drop everything to follow Jesus. But I wonder how Peter's family felt when he quit his job and deserted them for the sake of the gospel."

Challenge 8: Mobility and Uprootedness

One of the greatest stressors people experience involves moving across the country or across the state to accept a new position. While in times past pastors generally ministered within a particular geographical locale—for example, my father spent his entire ministry within a two-hour drive of the American Baptist Seminary of the West (then Berkeley Baptist Divinity School) in Berkeley, California, where he studied—pastors routinely accept calls that take them from one coast to the other. One of my best friends has just accepted a call in the Pacific Northwest. She feels called to this new pastoral position, but the move will take her away from her adult children and grandchildren. She is clear that she is seeking a new life for herself and her husband, but, as she admits, "I will miss seeing my children and grandchildren on a weekly basis. I'm looking forward to new forms of ministry, but I am already grieving the distance between us and the rest of the family." My friend's story is not unusual. As I shared the challenge of mobility with a pastor in her twenties, she noted that for younger pastors the challenge is often leaving home and truly being independent for the first time. She noted that "I visited my parents every week the first year on my day off just to have something familiar and stable in my life." Another young pastor noted the challenges of "beginning his first real job and learning what it meant to live on his own and set up a household apart from his parents or school settings." I resonate with the grief these pastors experience, having just accepted a pastoral call five hundred miles from grandchildren with whom I had regularly played several times each week.

Challenge 9. Postmodernism and Pluralism

Once upon a time the church was the only religious option for most North Americans. Sunday morning was sacred, stores were closed, and sporting events were delayed until after services concluded. The various streams of Christian theology and worship vied for the allegiance of potential members with little consideration for people of other faiths except as potential converts. Typically, people who were born Lutherans died Lutherans; cradle Episcopalians traversed the seasons of life without thinking of changing denominations; and Roman Catholics followed the pattern of confession, communion, and saints' days regardless of their feelings about the priest or papal leadership. All this has changed: denominational brand loyalty is a thing of the past as many people regularly change their denominational affiliation based on style of worship, quality of preaching, friendships, theology, social issues, and programmatic offerings. It is not unusual for people to grow up Presbyterian, attend a United Methodist church in college, raise their family in an independent church, and retire to a Disciples congregation. In the spirit of postmodernism, worshipers are looking for positive experiences and concrete theologies; they assume that no tradition has a corner on truth; they also believe that whatever speaks to them is the "right" faith community for this time in their lives. Only a minority of Christians take doctrine and ritual seriously in their congregational quests; what is important to many prospective church members is the right fit between my journey and a particular congregation's offerings. In describing the current spiritual landscape, a report from the Pew Forum on Religion and Public Life notes that 20 percent of North Americans have no institutional religious affiliation, and that this number increases to 30 percent among young adults. Moreover, many people practice spiritual techniques from a variety of religious traditions, often with little or no integration with their Christian faith: they attend worship on Sunday, go to a yoga or Tai Chi class on Tuesday, do breath prayer taught by Thich Nhat Hanh every morning, and find inspiration in best sellers by the Dalai Lama and Deepak Chopra. Anyone with an Internet connection and cable television can become versed in the various flavors of global spirituality. As a veteran United Methodist pastor noted, "I need to study regularly about new religious movements and popular spiritual teachers just to keep up with my congregants." Another pastor responded, "Many of my parishioners no longer feel the need to attend church regularly. If they can find wisdom on a Sunday morning by reading a Sufi teacher, the *Secret*, or a Zen Master, they'd just as soon have a few cups of coffee, sit by the fireplace, and read as attend church. It's frustrating that books and workshops have supplanted the real presence of Christ in Christian community."

Many pastors are intrigued and fascinated the growing number of people who refer to themselves as "spiritual but not religious."[3] While there is no clear definition of spirituality and practice among the self-described spiritual-but-not-religious, they find personal spirituality much more satisfying than the day-to-day complexities and challenges of congregational life and ongoing institutional commitment. They identify the church with institutional religion—doctrinaire, inflexible, hypocritical, mundane, and intolerant—and want little to do with structured and organized religion. In the spirit of postmodernism, spirituality is personal and experiential, something we make up as we go along and not tied to archaic traditionalism. The rise of unaffiliated, spiritual-but-not-religious people has made evangelism challenging for pastors. A thirtysomething Episcopalian pastor noted, "My mentors in ministry always made it a point to visit anyone who showed up for worship twice. If they came three or four times, they would approach them about joining the church. Today, if I made some of the same evangelistic moves, many young adults would run for their lives. They're cool with going to church and participating in a soup kitchen or Habitat for Humanity program, but the last thing they want to do is join something and make long-term spiritual commitments. The congregation wants numerical growth, but doesn't understand how everything has changed since the 1960s. I feel caught between responding to the spiritual styles of young adults—and sometimes their parents—and the old models of church membership, attendance, and stewardship."

Challenge 10. Dissonance between Vision and Reality

Most pastors entered ordained ministry inspired by a vision of spiritual leadership and personal transformation. The seminaries they attended encouraged them to see themselves as teachers, pastors, spiritual guides, social activists, and change agents. Although this is not unique to ministry—there are idealistic lawyers, teachers, and physicians too—many pastors have become disillusioned by the concrete messiness of congregational life and the inability of congregations to embrace the changes necessary to be faithful to the gospel. One frustrated Lutheran pastor noted, "I feel like a hospice chaplain. I came here expecting that people wanted this congregation to grow. I thought they would be interested in theology, spiritual practices, and outreach to the community. But, the most important issues I've faced involve the color of the carpet in the parlor and whether or not we should project the words of hymns, rather than use hymnals, in the worship service. When they get bogged down for weeks on the date of the annual church yard sale or the color of the parlor carpet, I get so frustrated that I want to shake them, look them in the eye, and shout, 'Is this what Jesus came for—the color of your damned carpet? Is this what the gospel's about—making sure vagrants don't sleep in the parking lot?'"

I suspect the tension between idealism and the realities of church life is nothing new among spiritual leaders. After all, the apostle Paul wrote, "Do not be conformed to this world, but be transformed by the renewing of your minds, so that you may discern what is the will [or vision] of God—what is good and acceptable and perfect" (Rom. 12:2). There has always been a dissonance between vision and reality in congregational life. But perhaps in no previous era has the embodiment of a lively Christian vision become more imperative as the North American church decreases numerically and, as a result, declines in its impact on and relevance to the broader society. With the fate of the planet at stake, many pastors are disillusioned by the insignificance of their congregation's most heated arguments and controversies. A Church of the Brethren pastor's laments echo those of the previously mentioned Lutheran pastor: "In seminary, I was told that theology, spiritual practices, and social change were at the heart of ministry. But here, if I put them ahead of what hymns to sing—you know, the battles between traditionalists and innovators—or whether we should repave the parking lot, my job will be in jeopardy. If I preach what I truly believe and tell them what they need to do to be faithful, I might as well start circulating my ministerial profile. The planet is in peril and the biggest deal around this church is whether or not to have an Easter egg hunt or reschedule the chicken and pancake dinner!"

A HEALING VISION FOR PASTORAL LEADERS

Ministry has always been challenging and potentially hazardous to the pastor and her or his family's health. Mark's Gospel notes that the pastoral needs Jesus's disciples faced were so great that "many were coming and going, and they had no leisure even to eat" (Mark 6:31). And this was before the Internet, iPhones, and instant messaging! In spite of the internal and external stresses of ministry, I believe that we can, in the spirit of Paul's letter to the Philippians, rejoice in our ministries and experience the joys of a healthy, dynamic, and creative life as pastors, partners, and parents.

My approach to self-care and ministerial excellence is health oriented. While congregational life and ministerial lifestyles are home to much pathology, they also bear witness to a gentle providence moving through our lives that has guided us from our births, energizing and inspiring us amid the quotidian events of daily life. As Paul says to the Philippians—and I proclaim this to every pastor—"The one who began a good work among you will bring it to completion by the day of Jesus Christ . . . the harvest of righteousness that comes through Jesus Christ for the glory and praise of God" (Phil. 1:6, 11). We nurture the good work of divine providence in our lives by our beliefs, lifestyle, spiritual practices, and relationships. Joy in ministry is not accidental but emerges in the dynamic interplay of call and response and grace and action that connect us with God's healing visions for us, our congregations, and the world. As one of my former students, now a Unitarian Universalist pastor, reminds me, ministerial joy emerges when we "trust that that the arc of the universe is bending toward good for all, including us."

What we believe can be a matter of life and death. It can inspire healthy or dysfunctional images and practices of ministry. Unhealthy ministerial practices find their impetus in the following theological assertions:

Salvation is a matter of merit and achievement rather than graceful empowerment. Our relationship with God depends entirely on our effectiveness in ministry.

We are on our own as professionals. Success and failure in ministry depends entirely on the quality of our efforts.

Body, mind, and spirit are unrelated. The quality of our spiritual life or ministerial effectiveness is unrelated to physical, emotional, and relational well-being.

We are indispensable in our ministerial leadership. The congregation cannot thrive without us.

Our call to ordained ministry separates us from our congregants.
Our call to spiritual leadership is unique in our congregations.

The call to ministry is our primary or sole vocation in relation to which every other relationship (self-care, family, or marriage) is subordinate.

Unhealthy theologies are ultimately graceless and dualistic. They separate us from others and alienate us from our own needs. Everything must be sacrificed for the sake of our ministerial calling. We believe that professional, not to mention personal, salvation is primarily the result our own efforts, and we feel that we are constantly being judged by God and others.

A healthy vision of ministry is grounded in a very different set of values and affirmations:

God is graceful and loving and is constantly moving in our lives, providing us with possibilities, synchronous encounters, and the energy to embody joyful and excellent ministry.

God's primary goal for us is abundant life. Divine judgment is educational rather than punitive and corrective rather than alienating. Divine judgment always exists in the context of God's unconditional and transformative love for us.

We live in a world of relationships. We are never alone but are always being sustained by God and others.

Mind, body, and spirit are dynamically interdependent and healthy, and excellent ministry involves caring for the temple of God's Spirit in every aspect of our lives.

As pastors we have many callings. God calls us to be caring and compassionate as parents, friends, partners and spouses, and pastors. God also calls us to care for ourselves so that we can be a blessing to others.

Within every congregation, there are as many vocations as congregants. While the pastor has a unique vocation as spiritual leader, caregiver, healer, teacher, and proclaimer of good news, everyone within the body of Christ is called to ministry for the common good.

Ministry is a partnership in which we strive as pastors to bring forth the vocational callings of others for the good of the church and the whole earth.

The healthy theological vision that undergirds my approach to ministerial self-care and excellence involves relationship, interdependence, and growth inspired and energized by the providence of a graceful God. Pastors are never alone, nor are we fated to repeat unhealthy professional patterns. We can open to God's creative transformation, supported by God's grace and the prayers and challenges of colleagues.

HEALTHY PRACTICES FOR HEALTHY PASTORS

Healthy and effective ministry involves the lively and evolving interplay of vision and practice. Throughout this text, I will provide a variety of spiritual practices for healthy pastors. Put simply, practices are behaviors that are essential to shaping our personal, relational, and professional lives in healthy ways. Practices bring us closer to God and others and promote personal and professional self-awareness. Practices enable us to consecrate the ordinary tasks of life as well as our long-term goals. A commitment to regular spiritual and relational practices nurtures health, wholeness, and effectiveness in ministry over a lifetime. When I began teaching medical students in the 1980s, I asked them the following question, "Will you still have joy and health in your professional lives twenty years from now?" This question has evolved in my conversations with seminarians and new pastors: "Will you have health and joy in your ministry twenty years from now? Will your spouse or partner, children, and companion animals be able to make the same affirmation about your ministry? Will it bring joy and health to their lives as well?"

Vision-oriented theology is not abstract and unrelated to real life; our theologies are intended to be practical and life transforming. Each chapter in this book presents a theological-spiritual practice or practices to promote healthy and excellent ministry. I invite you to live with each practice, letting its wisdom transform your way of doing ministry and your balance of professional, personal, and relational life.

As we begin our journey of healthy ministry, I invite you now as you finish this chapter to relax in a comfortable position—sitting in your easy chair, lying down, or in yoga position. Pause to notice your breath and to experience the quality of your overall well-being—body, mind, and spirit. How would you evaluate your physical, spiritual, emotional, and relational experience? Breathe gently and regularly, letting the energy of God's love flow in and through you. After five minutes of relaxing into God's care, take a moment to read the following words from Philippians 4:4–7:

Rejoice in the Lord always; again I will say, Rejoice. Let your gentleness be known to everyone. The Lord is near. Do not worry about anything, but in everything by prayer and supplication with thanksgiving let your requests be made known to God. And the peace of God, which surpasses all understanding, will guard your hearts and your minds in Christ Jesus.

Let these words soak in, permeating your body, mind, and spirit. Then read them again, opening yourself to their meaning for you. In the spirit of the Benedictine practice of lectio divina, or holy reading, reflect on what word or phrase speaks to your spirit today. How might you embody that word in your ministry and personal life? Take a few minutes to let the word or phrase become a prayer, and let your prayer join God's prayer for you. Throughout the day return to that prayer word for comfort, challenge, and guidance. Give thanks for the divine wisdom that guides your life and ministry.

2

DO YOU WANT TO BE MADE WELL?

Now in Jerusalem by the Sheep Gate there is a pool, called in He-
brew Beth-zatha, which has five porticoes. In these lay many inva-
lids—blind, lame, and paralyzed. One man was there who had been
ill for thirty-eight years. When Jesus saw him lying there and knew
that he had been there a long time, he said to him, "Do you want to
be made well?" The sick man answered him, "Sir, I have no one to
put me into the pool when the water is stirred up; and while I am
making my way, someone else steps down ahead of me." Jesus said to
him, "Stand up, take your mat and walk." At once the man was made
well, and he took up his mat and began to walk.

—John 5:2–9

BECOMING WELL

Do you want to be made well? These words reflect God's question to
many pastors today. These words are addressed to you in the complexities of ministry, relationships, and political and community involvement. God wants us to have abundant life in our ministries and relationships, but we often turn away from the very resources intended to give
us joy and abundance. We preach grace but believe that we have to
earn God's love by working tirelessly on our own and to the detriment
of our closest relationships. Many pastors are well aware that they are
running on empty, spending too many nights away from home, eating
too many meals on the run, and neglecting their spiritual lives and

physical well-being. But, despite recognizing that their habits are undermining their quality of life and ability to maintain long-term ministerial excellence, these pastors appear caught in a vicious cycle from which there appears to be no escape.

The good news is that harried and stressed pastors can become pilgrims on an upward spiral of wholeness. Pastors can repent their destructive lifestyles and turn toward God's vision of abundant life of body, mind, spirit, and relationships.

STRESS AS A BADGE OF HONOR

Have you ever been to a meeting of ministers in which the gathered pastors vie with one another about the stresses they experience in ministry? One pastor humorously related observing one such stressfest at a gathering of United Church of Christ pastors: "Prior to the ministerium meeting, a few of us chatted informally about current ministries. One pastor complained that she had five evening meetings last week and was completely worn out. Not to be outdone, another described a month with nine funerals, and how little time she had for sermon preparation. Still another proclaimed without blinking an eye that he had missed all of his children's soccer and baseball games this season because he had so much to do in building an excellent Sunday school and vacation church school program. Trumping them all, the final pastor boasted that he and his wife hadn't had a date in three months; things were so busy at church with the addition of a new education wing, capital campaign, and calling of a new associate pastor. I sat back and smiled at their stories of dysfunctional ministry. I knew if I mentioned that I took two days off a week and routinely limited myself to two night meetings a week, they would think I was some sort of ministerial slacker!" A Unitarian Universalist pastor surmised, "Sharing our stress is a badge of honor for many of us. Given the state of our congregations, we have so little else to boast of." What if instead of boasting of dysfunctional professional habits, pastors shared practices of health and wholeness in ministry? What if ministerial commitment was understood as balancing excellence in ministry with commitment to family, relationships, study, and self-care? What if pastors shared how they intentionally befriended time, reserving enough quality time for friends, family, and study while using their ministerial time effectively and efficiently?

In contrast to the health orientation at the heart of this book, I recall a conversation with Victoria, the pastor of a four-hundred-member United Methodist Church, in which she confessed, "I have only one speed in ministry and that's nonstop. I work until I drop." True to her confession, she fell ill every year on the weeks following Christmas and Easter. On the verge of wrecking her health and family life, she experienced a moment of insight: "I'm going to kill myself and destroy everything I love if I keep this up. I don't have to prove myself to God or my congregation anymore, and frankly I never ever had to. I can trust God to use my humble and imperfect efforts to further God's realm. It's not entirely up to me to bring about God's kingdom or grow this church. I need to let go of my need to be perfect and control things, and enable my church leaders to become partners in ministry." Victoria admits she occasionally backslides into a combination of workaholic, micromanaging, and overfunctioning behaviors. But Victoria now regularly exercises, takes twenty minutes each day for prayer and journaling, and limits her average work week to forty-five to fifty hours. She even takes a day off for recreation and a study day for sermon preparation, study, and prayer. Much to her surprise, she enthused, "My church is growing spiritually and numerically. And it's not about me. I do my part, but I am learning each day to trust the faithfulness of God and the gifts of my congregation. It's a relief not being 'goddess' around here anymore. Being pastor is good enough!" Pastors can experience healing and discover along the way that healthy spiritual and professional practices contribute to effectiveness and excellence in ministry. Time can be our friend; we don't have to be stress addicts but can consider the lilies, living out our personal, ministerial, and spiritual priorities one day at a time.

YOU CAN BE HEALED!

The encounter of Jesus and the man at the pool provides many insights for overworked and overwhelmed pastors. When Jesus asks him if he wants to be healed, the man doesn't respond with an immediate and unambiguous yes as we might expect. Instead, he states what keeps him from getting well. He places his healing in the hands of others, rather than claiming responsibility for his own well-being. No doubt there is truth in the reasons he gives; but focusing on the external reasons for his illness only serves to exacerbate his passivity and paralysis. He looks for a special moment to transform life—an angelic visitation or the impact of some other external source—when the resources he needs for healing are right in front of him and within him.

Jesus, however, refuses to let the man define himself by his excuses and limitations. Jesus imagines him standing up and healthy once again, an agent in his own personal transformation. He challenges him to become an actor in his own life, choosing moment by moment, beginning right now, to shape his own destiny. God's grace, embodied in Jesus's relentless quest for wholeness, inspires our agency and freedom to change our lives. "Stand up, take up your mat and walk," Jesus commands. In following Jesus, the man claims his power and ability to move forward in his life, unimpeded by previous physical and spiritual limitations.

Still, claiming a healthy way of life is a process and not a destination. We never entirely have it together, and every so often we fall into bad habits or return to unhealthy professional practices. Even after he stands up and begins to walk, the once-paralyzed man is immediately tempted to backslide, putting his well-being at risk by his passivity; he tells the religious teachers that Jesus made him carry his bed instead of responding, "Jesus healed me, and now I'm carrying my bed, rejoicing in my new life, even if it is the Sabbath." Jesus is compelled to address the man once more, this time reminding him that his well-being is a personal decision that must be reaffirmed one moment at a time. In words that can be misunderstood when taken out of context, Jesus advises him, "See, you have been made well! Do not sin any more so that nothing worse happens to you!" (v. 14). Jesus's counsel is not intended to be threatening, nor does Jesus assume divine punishment for the man's passivity. He is challenging him to claim his newfound well-being. Perhaps, his passivity was a source of his paralysis. Now that he can walk, he must choose to walk one step at a time.

IMPEDIMENTS TO MINISTERIAL SELF-CARE

Do you want to be made well? This is the first and foremost question for pastors seeking to be healthy and whole. Many pastors know only too well the inner conflicts Paul describes in his own quest for spiritual integrity. We are addicted to our professional lifestyles, despite their unhealthy impact on our lives, ministries, and relationships. Only grace can deliver us from addictions that imprison us. Listen to the apostle Paul's struggles to claim God's new and abundant life:

> For I do not do what I want, but I do the very thing I hate. . . . For I
> do not do the good I want but the evil I do not want is what I do.
> —Romans 7:15, 19

As one United Methodist pastor related, "I know I need to practice a healthier lifestyle and take time off from ministry, but I fall back into old habits before I know it and end up back where I started from. It's easier to eat fast food and be a couch potato. Healthy eating and daily exercise take effort." A Southern Baptist pastor admitted, "I never realized how difficult it is to change your ministerial style. I still get stuck in bad habits, like working too hard and trying to please everyone. I don't maintain healthy boundaries in terms of time and availability to congregants. In fact, my bad habits are considered socially acceptable. My congregants and colleagues see them as signs of commitment to the church. My ministerial style gets in the way of being the minister, husband, and father I feel called to be. My style gets in the way of being faithful to Jesus." These pastors along with many of their peers need a "come to Jesus" moment in which they move from halfheartedness, hiding from healing by invoking excuses, to spiritual, physical, and professional healing as they respond, "Yes, I want to be healed, and I'm ready to change my life to receive the healing God wants for me and my vocation as pastor."

Barbara Brown Taylor's *Leaving Church* is a testimony to how difficult it is for pastors to embrace abundant life in ministry. Taylor moves from an urban church to a country parish to reclaim the wellsprings of vital and healthy ministry. Her first wake-up call came when she discovered that she no longer noticed the beauty all around her. In a moment of introspection, Taylor asks what's preventing her from experiencing the beauty she so desperately needs to nurture her spiritual and physical well-being:

> Why did I seal myself off from all this freshness? On what grounds did I fast myself from the daily bread of birdsong and starlight? The obvious answer was that I was a priest, with more crucial things to do than to go for a walk around the park. I had been blessed with work so purposeful that taking time off from it felt like a betrayal of divine trust.[1]

Sadly, a change in scenery does not lead to a change in lifestyle and attitude. Increasingly burdened and on the verge of burnout, she discovers that "the demands of ministry routinely cut me off from the resources that enabled me to do parish ministry. I knew where God's fire was burning, but I could not get to it."[2] Although she appeared to all observers to be an exemplary pastor, Taylor felt increasingly spiritually and emotionally depleted. She confesses:

> I had moved to the country to live closer to the Divine Presence that held me all my life, but I had once again become so busy caring for the household of God that I neglected the one who called me there. If I still had plenty of energy for work, that was because feeding others was still my food. As long as I fed them, I did not feel my own hunger pains.[3]

Unable and unwilling to transform her life, Taylor ultimately left congregational ministry. Although Taylor's story has a happy ending—she finds a new profession and with it notoriety—not all pastors fare so well. They succumb to burnout, alienation from family, and professional mediocrity and, on occasion, sickness, unemployment, or misconduct as a result of their unhealthy professional lifestyles.

Beneath Taylor's tale of dysfunctional ministry, however, is an invitation to pastors on the verge of burnout: you don't have to conform to unhealthy ministerial habits; you can respond to God's call toward wholeness. You can choose to become well. You can be healed and claim your role as a healing partner with others.

WHAT KEEPS YOU AT THE POOLSIDE?

When Jesus asked the man with paralysis if he wanted to be made well, his response was perfectly reasonable—I'm all alone and no one helps me get in the pool when the healing angel appears. His legitimate response challenges us to examine our ministerial lifestyles and with it our self-imposed impediments to wellness in our personal and professional lives.

Take a moment to consider the following questions: What are your reasons for continuing ministerial and personal practices you know to be detrimental to your overall health and ministerial effectiveness? What keeps you from following Jesus's advice, "Stand up; take up your mat and walk?" Answering these questions honestly may be the first step in your own process of standing up to move forward in healthy ministry.

I asked a group of high-functioning pastors individually and on Facebook the following questions: What are the personal impediments that keep you from practicing a healthy ministry? How would you respond to Jesus's question, Do you want to be made well? Do you want to be a healthy pastor? The responses were honest and insightful and reflected each pastor's personal theology, spirituality, and self-awareness.

Francis, a Unitarian Universalist pastor living on the Eastern Seaboard, confessed, "I'm afraid to change. I'm comfortable with the way I do ministry and know that opting for a healthier lifestyle would mean big changes. I'd have to say no to my congregants' demands, I'd have to let go of perfectionism, and I'd have to let others pick up the slack and live with their imperfections. I know I'm working too hard, but if I let go of control, I'm afraid that our ministries will suffer, and I don't want that to happen! I guess I'm a control freak, but what does this say about my attitude toward my congregants? And what does this say about my attitude toward ministry? Do I really have all this power and am I using it in a good way?"

Steve, an Episcopalian priest in Southern California, revealed that "I'm a people pleaser. I want my congregation to like me and if that means going the second mile and then another one after that, I'll do it. My partner's frustrated with all the time I spend away from home, but I'm afraid of making waves in the church. I want them to like me even if I have to pull my punches in sermons and meetings and cater to the big givers. If I'm no longer nice and pliable, I'm afraid they won't like me anymore, and that will be devastating." I talked to Steve several months later. After returning to therapy and spiritual direction, he discovered that there was something more important than being "nice"; it was being faithful—to God, to his ordination, and to his relationships.

Another pastor expressed a different kind of fear. Susan, the first woman to pastor in the two-hundred-year history of a New England American Baptist congregation, admitted that "following a series of workaholic male pastors, two of whom actually died of heart attacks while serving this church, I'm afraid of being seen as weak. The people cherished these pastors; they actually saw them as ideal ministers who sacrificed everything for Christ and they want me to do the same thing. I feel like I'm bearing the burden of being the first woman pastor here. I wonder if my predecessors really worked around the clock and sacrificed their health out of fidelity to Christ. Could it have been lack of vocational imagination or fear of letting go of control? I wonder if they could imagine another way to do ministry. Just talking with you, Bruce, is a wakeup call: I'm not Jesus, and I sure don't want to be these guys. I don't need to sacrifice my life for the church. I want to live and be a good mother and wife. Hey, even Jesus took time off to pray, eat out, and party."

Similar to Susan, Eduardo confessed to being afraid of "letting my parishioners know I'm human." This Presbyterian pastor averred, "I know it's stupid. But, I don't want them to see me sweat or look anxious, and so I put on a front. I want them to think I'm the omnicompetent, supereffective, and ever-present pastor. If I get sick, cancel meetings, or admit my stresses, I fear they'll recognize my weaknesses and lose their respect for me. Last winter I was sick as a dog two Sundays and still preached. What does that say about me and my understanding of grace?"

I recently saw a bumper sticker in the Claremont School of Theology parking lot that proclaimed, "Jesus is coming. Look busy!" Every minister has heard, much to her or his chagrin, a congregant tell the following joke: "You have an easy life. You only work an hour a week!" No doubt pastors feel the need to prove their importance to the church and want to make sure their congregants know how involved they are in church and community activities. In our culture one of the best ways to seem indispensable is to show up everywhere, be part of everything, and look busy whenever people are there to observe. I recall hearing of an old-school Central Pennsylvania Reformed pastor who took a vacation only three times in thirty years in his Pennsylvania congregation. He believed that God called him to ministry and that was the most important thing in life, more important than marriage, family, and health. As I heard the story being told by his successor, I wondered if the previous pastor was afraid that God and his congregants might somehow get along without him if he took a holiday!

Thad, a Cooperative Baptist Convention pastor, blames the value system of his seminary education. Over a cup of coffee and scones, he noted, "In seminary we were taught to be workaholics. I wanted to fit into the mold of being the self-sacrificial pastor. I'm serving in Christ's place. I have to work, for night is coming, as the hymn goes." However, after hearing his explanation, Thad responded, "I guess I can't blame the seminary or the church entirely. After I left seminary, I still followed the counsel of my teachers and fellow students. I don't have to anymore. I can choose to be both healthy and effective." Pastors are rewarded for being self-sacrificial and taking up their cross. Many pastors feel they have to justify taking time off for study, family life, or self-care. Some discover, quite ironically, that their congregations have known all along that their pastor's self-sacrificial behavior was self-destructive. They've just been waiting for the right moment to tell their pastor to slow down and spend more time at home.

Today's pastors, like their congregants, are aware of suffering in the world. Unlike many of their congregants, they also have firsthand experience of the hidden tragedies within their congregations. Toby confided that he was so overwhelmed by his congregants' pain that he often emotionally shuts down. "The pain is so great, and in this church, folks are dealing with incurable illness, job loss, substance abuse, loneliness and grief, and foreclosure. There's always so much to do, and the need is unending. I could work night and day, and sometimes I do, and not make a dent in world hunger, sex trafficking, racism, and the pain in my own congregation. Sometimes I'm glad I'm single. I don't know if I'd ever have time enough for marriage. But when I come home and have a couple of glasses of Scotch to unwind, I feel lonely some nights."

The tasks of ministry are never ending, and the best we can do is respond to them one task at a time. The work will always be unfinished. When we are tempted to go it alone or to try to earn God's love by our achievements, we need to remember that God's gentle providence is at work supplementing and energizing our own efforts. One of the greatest spiritual leaders of the early Christian movement recognized that although God does not demand our submission, God works creatively through our fallibility and imperfection. Struggling with his own finitude and weakness, Paul places his trust in God's wise companionship: "My grace is sufficient for you, for power is made perfect in weakness" (2 Cor. 12:9). Paul is affirming the grace of interdependence and the power that comes when we become partners in God's providence mediated through spiritual resources and faithful friends. Connected with grace, we can be high-functioning and healthy pastors, aware of our limits, taking time for self-care, and awakening to the grace that guides and energizes.

CLAIMING HEALTHY MINISTRY

Do you want to be well? Do you want a dynamic, healthy, and flexibly balanced ministry that honors your many callings—pastor, parent, child, spouse, partner, self, citizen, and so forth? Claiming a healthy ministry is a theological and spiritual issue as well as a matter of professional conduct. Take a moment to consider the following questions: What is your working theology of ministry? In the words of the Reformers, is your ministry a reflection of works righteousness or faith in a graceful God?

Jesus invoked three interdependent commandments as guides for spiritual well-being and transformation: "You shall love the Lord your God with all your heart, and with all your soul, and with all your mind, and with all your strength. . . . You shall love your neighbor as yourself" (Mark 12:30–31).

While love of God centers our love for ourselves and others, in truth we cannot fully love God without joining healthy self-affirmation with loving care for others. We do not have to choose between loving the creatures and loving the creator, and loving others and loving ourselves. In fact, we love the creator best by loving God's creation, and that means loving ourselves. This is the heart of Mother Teresa's quest to "do something beautiful for God."

If God is omnipresent, then the whole earth is full of God's glory. Every person, place, and moment reveals God's presence and vision. God is not an indifferent force, amoral and unconcerned with the world; rather God's goal for your life is congruent with Jesus's mission statement: "I came that they [all God's beloved] may have life, and have it abundantly" (John 10:10). Neither divine omnipresence nor God's vision of abundant life is a theological abstraction. In this very moment, God wants you to have abundant life in the many aspects of your life. God wants everyone else to have abundant life as well. Concretely speaking, God seeks abundance, wholeness, beauty, and healing in every moment and situation. The shape of God's vision is embodied contextually; it is always at work right where you are. Within the limitations of your current life situation, including your healthy and unhealthy professional and personal habits, your prayer life, your addictions, and your deep desire for wholeness, God is at work, providing creative possibilities and the energy to embody them in daily life.

To those pastors who feel stressed-out, overworked, and trapped in unhealthy professional behaviors, the good news is that God wants you to be well. God is on your side and speaking to you in "sighs too deep for words" (Rom. 8:26). As Jesus's ministry proclaims, God calls us all to the personal transformation that is essential to claiming our role as God's partners in healing the world. God wants us as pastors to love ourselves enough to care for ourselves. We don't have to earn this grace; it is ours to experience and claim. Loving ourselves means that we can stand up spiritually, like the man at the pool, inspired and guided by God to say yes to practices of healthy ministry and relatedness and to say no to behaviors and attitudes that undermine our well-being, even when they come from the church.

HEALTHY PRACTICES FOR HEALTHY PASTORS

The first step toward experiencing healing and wholeness and embodying self-care that reflects God's passion for abundant life is to pause long enough to listen to your deepest yearnings expressed in your dreams, physical condition, vocational possibilities, and passions. The psalmist proclaims, "Be still and know that I am God!" (Ps. 46:10). One translation of the words "be still" is "pause awhile."

Take some time each day to begin the habit of pausing in God's presence to experience the uniqueness of your life. Find a comfortable spot in an easy chair, a yoga position, or even lying down, and simply "listen to your life," as theologian and author Frederick Buechner suggests. Notice the quality of your breath, your sense of well-being or disease, your overall physical well-being, your current emotional and spiritual condition. In the stillness, simply listen for the "sighs too deep for words" revealed through your cells as well as your spirit. Let your whole being speak to you, perhaps for the first time, in its pain and wisdom.

Following the wisdom of author and educator Parker Palmer, take a moment to "let your life speak." Ask yourself, what is the deepest desire of my heart today? Deep down, our deepest desires reflect what Augustine describes as the restlessness of heart, which lures us to the fullness that comes from being in relationship with God's vision for us. Listen without any attempt to edit the words and images that emerge.

After a few moments, ask yourself, and God moving within yourself, what one step can I take today to experience God's healing of mind, body, spirit, relationships, and ministry? Listen for the guidance of the Spirit's whispers within you. If you receive any wisdom at this time, conclude with a prayer of commitment to embody the wisdom you have experienced. If nothing tangible emerges at this time, ask for further guidance and wisdom to find healing and wholeness for yourself and for those with whom you live and minister.

The prophet Habakkuk counsels, "Write the vision. Make it plain on tablets" (Hab. 2:2). Habakkuk's wisdom is central to personal and professional growth as well as congregational vitality. In this spirit, take a few minutes to journal your time of personal reflection. Journaling grounds what we have experienced in the concreteness and fluidity of language and serves as a reminder and guidepost on our pilgrimage of pastoral wholeness, excellence, and self-care.

3

LIVING BY ABUNDANCE IN A TIME OF SCARCITY

When he looked up and saw a large crowd coming toward him, Jesus said to Philip, "Where are we to buy bread for these people to eat?" He said this to test him, for he himself knew what he was going to do. Philip answered him, "Six months' wages would not buy enough bread for each of them to get a little." One of his disciples, Andrew, Simon Peter's brother, said to him, "There is a boy here who has five barley loaves and two fish. But what are they among so many people?" Jesus said, "Make the people sit down." Now there was a great deal of grass in the place; so they sat down, about five thousand in all. Then Jesus took the loaves, and when he had given thanks, he distributed them to those who were seated; so also the fish, as much as they wanted.

—John 6:5–11

A DEEPER REALISM OR SCARCITY THINKING

Ed came home frustrated again after the church council meeting. This Presbyterian congregation of seven hundred members needed to expand its program staff to respond to a growing community of young families and children, but once again the church council balked. The growing congregation had turned the corner on stagnation and was moving forward under Ed's leadership, but the current staff, as they responded to the resulting demands, was overworked and overprogrammed with no end in sight. "What's with these people?" Ed complained to his wife. "The congregation's growing, the budget's up, but they are afraid they might go into the red again. This doesn't make sense when they have more than $500,000 in unrestricted endowment and $1,000,000 more that's restricted but can be used to support special projects. I understand fiscal responsibility, but they're thinking too small. We need to spend a little from our savings to have a topnotch program." A lot of pastors would love to have Ed's complaints: after all, his church is growing and has funds in reserve.

A midwestern Disciples of Christ pastor, Sheldon tells a far different story, one that could be repeated in thousands of congregations today. "The people in my church constantly are looking at the budget and savings and wondering how much longer do we have? They're tired and feel old, and some are really worried about closing the doors if things don't turn around in the next few years. They're depressed and I'm starting to feel depressed too!" Santiago echoes the same sentiment from the vantage point of his inner-city United Methodist church: "We're always under the threat of closure, and we're scared. We think our finances will save us. We have a lovely building, a good endowment, but only fifty in a church sanctuary that once held five hundred. They don't want to spend a penny on outreach or mission. It seems like every time the board talks about money, we sound like we're on our own, alone in the world, with no God to hear our prayers." This is a pattern everywhere these days: I will be consulting with a congregation next week as it decides to move from full-time to part-time leadership. I am hoping that at this time they won't see staff reductions as a sign of imminent death but—despite big challenges—as an opportunity for a new kind of partnership between a bivocational pastor and an active laity.

Do you remember the story of the encounter of Elijah and the widow of Zarapheth (1 Kings 17:7–16)? When the prophet asks her for a piece of bread she responds, "As the LORD your God lives, I have nothing baked, only a handful of meal in a jar, and a little oil in a jug; I am now gathering a couple of sticks, so that I may go home and prepare it for myself and my son, that we may eat it, and die" (v. 12). Now that's scarcity thinking! I've heard similar statements from anxious pastors and lay leaders who see no future but slow decline and eventual death in their congregations.

Issues of scarcity are shaping the face of pastoral ministry. In light of the realities of congregational finances, many pastors are facing a crisis in compensation. They feel called to congregational ministry, but the congregations they love are struggling to pay a living wage, housing allowance, and medical and retirement benefits. A small-town, United Methodist pastor, Darrell admits that "right now, I'm beginning to feel desperate. I want to stay here, but I can barely make ends meet. Help!" Stephanie feels the same way. When she moved to a larger Presbyterian congregation in an urban area, she thought that her $20,000 pay increase would be sufficient, but she has discovered otherwise. Like Oscar, another urban pastor cited in the introductory chapter, she confesses, "I'm having a rough time of it. My husband's still looking for work, and although my salary and housing allowance amount to over $80,000, that doesn't go far when your mortgage, taxes, and utilities amount to $2,500 a month. I took another look at the demographics of the congregation and realized that the average family income is nearly $150,000 and that our income is in the bottom 25 percent. I'm praying hard for my husband to get a job and for us to get out of debt. I know I have First World worries, but I'm worried anyway and it takes a toll on my quality of life and ministry."

The question of pastoral compensation becomes even more crucial when a newly ordained pastor is also carrying a $20,000 to $40,000 debt from seminary and anticipates a starting salary of less than $50,000 including housing or $35,000 with a parsonage. This disparity hits both single and married pastors, not to mention clergy couples and bivocational pastors, who may be carrying more than $60,000 in debt or have left secure positions to follow God's call. Dennis and Sally, a United Church of Christ clergy couple, admit, "We really sweated out the search and call process. We needed two churches and two salaries and hoped that we could start up around the same time. We also needed to be within an hour's drive to care for our children and keep our relationship fresh." Sally was the first to receive a call; in her case, to a county-seat church in Ohio. She feels blessed to have a parsonage. She quips, "At least, we won't be homeless and without electricity if we can't pay the bills." But Sally's blessing becomes a problem for Dennis since many of the congregations with whom he interviewed were equally adamant about wanting their pastor living in a parsonage and could not afford the extra compensation for housing. Dennis laments, "Her blessing was my curse. We felt like we were between a rock and a hard place. Finally, though, I was called to a congregation that was comfortable with my commute and renting the manse to others. I'm elated, but it's ninety minutes away. Sometimes after a late night meeting, I just sleep on the couch in the pastor's study. I don't like the commute and miss tucking the kids in every night, but I feel called to this church and I've found I like to listen to audiobooks on my long drives."

I recently preached the sermon at the ordination of one of my former Lancaster Theological Seminary students. She had chosen Ezekiel 37:1–14 as one of the passages for the service. In an encounter with God, Ezekiel has a vision of a valley of dry bones and asks the telling question, "Can these dry bones live?" That's our question too as we look at the spiritual landscape and the current shape of Christianity. In our pluralistic, postmodern, and post-Christian North America, mainstream and many evangelical denominations are in deep trouble, congregations are losing members, and budgets and reserves are shrinking. In many ways, we are financially and numerically in very bad shape and have more of the same to look forward to in light of aging memberships and the changing spiritual and giving patterns of young people. It is absolutely essential to be realistic about our current situation. The current realities of congregational life cannot be denied or evaded—we must be realistic about budgets, expenditures, deficits, and memberships—but we must not confuse realism with scarcity. The biblical tradition speaks of a deeper realism, grounded in the synergy of divine and human transformation, which is able even to revive dry bones in the valley.

Still, the realities of congregational budgets and pastoral compensation can be disheartening and depressing for pastors and congregants alike. Many pastors see no way out of these limits except through looking for larger, better-paying churches or trying to find a cottage industry on the side. Both of these are increasingly difficult in the current economy and ministerial job market in which many pastors who had planned to retire between ages sixty-five and sixty-seven are now planning to work till seventy. Claiming abundant life is necessary for healthy ministry, but it isn't easy, especially when the limitations appear to be intractable in nature.

AWAKENING TO A DEEPER REALISM: A PASTORAL INTERLUDE

The Quakers have a saying "A way will be made." A variation of this affirmation is the statement "God makes a way where there is no way." Out of apparent scarcity, abundance emerges. Where there appears to be a dead end, a path appears. When we hit bottom, we discover God is with us and we can, in God's companionship, climb out of the mess in which we've found ourselves. When we think we are unlovable or will never find a loving friendship or partner, we have a synchronous meeting and everything changes.

There are no guarantees that Christians and people of other spiritual traditions will have an easy go of it. Pastoral ministry is challenging these days and the results of our labors are often influenced by factors beyond our control; moreover, the visions toward which we aspire may be deferred for years. Still, we may discover a highway in the desert, a path in the wilderness, and a polestar on the darkest night.

Jesus said that he came that we might have abundant life, and his ministry was a testimony to God's abundance, which invites us to balance the concrete realism of everyday life, budgets, bottom lines, and cultural trends with the deeper realism of divine inspiration and possibility. The first Christians heard these words as a vision of hope in God as they faced their own personal, financial, and social limitations. Excellence in ministry requires realism. We need to know the concrete realities of our personal and congregational finances to move ahead creatively. We need to be fiscally responsible, live within our means, and take prudent risks to achieve our goals. But scarcity thinking assumes that we are alone and without resources. It assumes that our actual situation cannot be altered or that our current financial or personal situation completely determines the future. In other words, scarcity thinking is guided by a practical atheism that implicitly assumes God is absent, unconcerned, or opposed to our flourishing. In contrast, I believe the biblical tradition describes a deeper realism, fully cognizant of limitation but open to divine inspiration, creativity, and energy. It assumes that we are never alone: God is with us, and in partnership with other people of faith, our lives and congregations can be transformed.

Five loaves and two fishes can't feed more than a few children; a little grain and oil will provide dinner with no leftovers for a widow and her son; a night of unsuccessful fishing means food rationing at home. But with God a way is made: a multitude is fed, a family survives a famine, and deeper waters yield a plentiful catch.

A story is told of Mother Teresa of Calcutta. When she proposed to begin a ministry of care for the homeless and dying, her superiors realistically asked, "How much money do you have?" Teresa responded, "A few pennies." They rejoined, "With a few pennies, you can't do anything." To which Teresa responded, "With two pennies and God, I can do anything!" This is not a manipulative prosperity gospel or New Age "create your own reality by positive thinking," but the recognition that within the limitations of life, possibilities emerge. A way will be made because Christ is the way maker.

Tony, a Progressive Baptist pastor, finds abundance at the communion table. He asserts that "every time we partake in communion at the Lord's abundant table we are celebrating God's providing for our deepest needs. When we share in the bread and cup, we proclaim resurrection life and take a stand against the materialistic ideologies of scarcity that breed poverty and greed." Susan, a Disciples of Christ pastor, agrees with Tony's eucharistic affirmation: "When we gather around the table, as we do in our fifty-member church, we don't feel alone and we don't feel small. Somehow we know we're connected to a greater love and a greater source. Every time I feel low, I go to the table, and I remind my congregation that our future isn't just in our efforts but in Jesus's life, death, and resurrection! That changes everything."

Sheryl, an African Methodist Episcopal (AME) pastor, sees abundance in the body of Christ. "When I feel worried about the future, I'm tempted to isolate myself from people. I know how important going into my closet for prayer time is, but sometimes I also need to reach out to brothers and sisters in the body of Christ. When I hear their voices or feel their touch, I know we're going to make it. Alone I'm lost, but together we shall be victorious."

One of my former students, Paula, expressed her gratitude for the support she experienced after her husband's death. "The love of family and friends has sustained me these last few months. I've realized that in the midst of grief, God's abundant grace has given me a new awareness and confidence in things I've been able to do, and thought I couldn't."

Another former student, Macrina, following a challenging time in her life, affirms, "God's grace has been providential in the tough times . . . a friend who calls at just the right time, a healing meal, a new poem to fall in love with, the sun shining and feeling that warmth, . . . and also the ability to be there for others and the opportunity to feel compassion."

We need creative antidotes to scarcity thinking, and this means taking chances on provocative possibilities, launching out into deeper waters, reaching out to companions in the body of Christ, and claiming God's nearness. We need to live by our affirmations, such as the New Creed from the United Church of Canada, as we discover God's way forward being made.

> We are not alone,
>   we live in God's world.
> We believe in God:
>   who has created and is creating,
>   who has come in Jesus,
>   the Word made flesh,
>   to reconcile and make new,
>   who works in us and others
>   by the Spirit.
> We trust in God.
> We are called to be the Church:
>   to celebrate God's presence,
>   to live with respect in Creation,
>   to love and serve others,
>   to seek justice and resist evil,
>   to proclaim Jesus, crucified and risen,
>   our judge and our hope.
> In life, in death, in life beyond death,
>   God is with us.
> We are not alone.
>   Thanks be to God.[1]

LIVING BY ABUNDANCE

In responding to my queries about scarcity and abundance, a United Methodist pastor wrote under the condition of anonymity, "I'm at a church that constantly looks at the budget as scarcity. We live by the principle we'll never have what we need and we shouldn't spend money unless it's truly necessary. There's a chart in the PowerPoint every Sunday showing how far below our budget we are each week. I was once at a church that created a budget and put as a line item 'God will provide,' and every year God did provide. That church believed in abundance not scarcity."

What we believe makes a tremendous difference in how we interpret our personal and congregational circumstances. David, an AME Zion pastor, proclaims, "I find abundance in gratitude. When I recall how much God has done for me, how he's come through in tight spots, and made a way, I know that it's going to be alright. I tell my congregation to count our blessings and out of gratitude, we will find that God will supply our needs. This isn't superficial prosperity gospel but trust in God's overarching providence to supply our deepest needs."

Living by abundance is a matter of a larger vision and deeper realism. A church fund-raiser once told me that he regularly asks congregations embarking on capital campaigns the question, what are you worth? Usually the church leaders and pastor talk about the value of the building, assets, pledges, endowment, and money on hand. He responds, "That's not what I'm asking. I want to know what you imagine the total financial worth of every family in this congregation is, the gifts of congregants, and your contribution to the community." He notes, "When they look at the big picture, they recognize that they have more assets than they imagined, but it's a matter of priorities and stewardship. It's a matter of having a congregational vision and investing in it."

Scarcity is real. Many congregations are in trouble and many pastors have difficulty making ends meet. The challenge of scarcity thinking is that it constricts our vision at precisely the time we need to be imaginative. The world can shrink to the size of the next budget meeting, our monthly paycheck, or a hospital room. Somehow, we need to awaken to God's possibilities amid the real limits we and our congregations face.

There is no one surefire antidote to scarcity thinking, nor will our changed practices or perspectives always insure success. However, a transformed mind can inspire us to actions that eventually transform our congregational and professional circumstances. In the next section, we explore practices that can enable you to experience God's abundant life in the midst of scarcity. As I've said earlier, healthy ministry is not the result of denying or evading life's difficulties but of committing yourself to creative and imaginative thinking and action.

HEALTHY PRACTICES FOR HEALTHY PASTORS

Healthy spiritual practices open us to places where God is at work in our lives and the world. They support our well-being in body, mind, and spirit and promote self-care in its broadest personal and vocational sense. While our personal practices are often conducted in solitude, they connect us with God and others; they remind us that we are not alone, we live in God's world.

Gratitude and Abundance

Gratitude is essential to spiritual well-being. When we are grateful, we discover that we are connected to a wellspring of possibilities that liberate us from the loneliness and isolation of scarcity thinking. The exercise that follows here can be practiced by a congregation as well as an individual person.

Find a comfortable place.

Center yourself by breathing gently and opening to the life-giving powers of breath.

Without prioritizing, begin noting the people and events for which you are grateful. Imagine each one, focusing on how you have been enriched and sustained.

Give thanks for each blessing as it emerges in your consciousness.

Make a prayer of thanksgiving, opening to the Giver of All Good Things.

You may choose to create a gratitude journal as a daily reminder of God's "great faithfulness" and the "new mercies" that come to us with each new day.

I believe that movement is important in healthy spirituality and in inspiring new ways of looking at the world. In that spirit, I invite you to take a gratitude walk, letting your gratitude for God's blessings rise up as you enjoy moving through your neighborhood or a place of beauty.

Scarcity thinking constricts our imaginations; movement, by nature, expands our vision of possibilities and inspires energy for their achievement.

Practicing Generosity

There is a dynamic connection between giving and receiving. Martin Luther described Christian freedom as the lived experience of being a "little Christ," sharing the grace he or she received with others. Today we might describe this as being as a channel of blessing. Scarcity thinking turns us inward, closing us off both as givers and as receivers; we focus simply on survival and not giving and receiving the blessings of life. Generosity is not magic, but my experience is that when I reach out to others in sharing time, talent, or treasure, my heart and mind expand. I no longer feel trapped by limitation but am opened to future possibilities.

In a spirit of prayer, ask God to show you where you can best share your time, talents, and treasure to promote God's vision of shalom in your neighborhood and the world. Ask God to give you a generous spirit to reach out to people in your daily life with encouragement and care.

Living by Affirmations

Living with Philippians 4 can transform your life.[2] I believe that Paul intends Philippians 4:4–9 to be a catalog of spiritual practices that enable us to experience God's good work in our lives coming to fulfillment. Meditate on these words as they relate to your current challenges:

> Rejoice in the Lord always; again I will say, Rejoice. [5]Let your gentleness be known to everyone. The Lord is near. [6]Do not worry about anything, but in everything by prayer and supplication with thanksgiving let your requests be made known to God. [7]And the peace of God, which surpasses all understanding, will guard your hearts and your minds in Christ Jesus.
>
> Finally, beloved, whatever is true, whatever is honorable, whatever is just, whatever is pure, whatever is pleasing, whatever is commendable, if there is any excellence and if there is anything worthy of praise, think about these things. [9]Keep on doing the things that you

have learned and received and heard and seen in me, and the God of peace will be with you.

Filled with profound spiritual insights about the interplay of joy, grati- tude, and prayer, this passage also invites us to transform our minds by "think[ing] about these things," about the affirmative and positive rath- er than the negative. In times of scarcity, images of fear often dominate our experience. While concern about congregational and personal fi- nances is essential, we often find ourselves mired in negativity, power- lessness, and hopelessness. We forget that we are connected to the vine of loving relationships and a loving God. Affirmations focus our minds and energize our actions. As if to remind us of the power of affirmative faith, the apostle follows his words about "think[ing] about" things of excellence with two great affirmations:

I can do all things through [Christ] who strengthens me.

—Philippians 4:13

And my God will fully satisfy every need of yours according to his riches in glory in Christ Jesus.

—Philippians 4:19

When we live with affirmations such as these, our external circum- stances don't immediately change, but our attitude changes sometimes immediately and always over time. We feel greater agency and free- dom, and new ideas come to us that can transform how we respond to our current situation. A new attitude can change the world by opening us to new possibilities.

Reaching Out

Relationship is everything in healthy ministry, and by that I mean rela- tionship with God, your close friends, family, and sources of help. When Jesus advised ask, seek, knock, I think he was referring both to prayer and to people in our lives. James 4:2 proclaims that "you do not have, because you do not ask." When we are in most need of divine and human help, we often turn inward, thinking we can go it alone. No one's resources are sufficient in a time of scarcity. It takes a village of friends, family, and professional companions to help us find our way. I know the need for reaching out firsthand. As I wrote the first draft of this text, I was currently exploring new ways of ministry through integrating writing, speaking, teaching, and pastoral ministry. I was also exploring possibilities in congregational ministry. Now that I have been called to congregational ministry on Cape Cod, I continue to reach out for collegial support in areas of faith formation and best practices in ministry. I have come to realize that when a possibility comes my way, I need to pick up the phone and contact my circle of professional friends to ask for their support. They often have wisdom, insight, and connections that are essential to furthering my professional vision. I've worked hard to feel comfortable asking for introductions and counsel. Now it's as easy as picking up the phone or sending an e-mail. I am asking for help, but I am also, in the interdependence of life, inviting my professional friends to be channels of blessing, growing spiritually through their own generosity.

4

TRANSFORMING TECHNOLOGY

Above all, clothe yourselves with love, which binds everything together in perfect harmony. And let the peace of Christ rule in your hearts, to which indeed you were called in the one body. And be thankful. Let the word of Christ dwell in you richly; teach and admonish one another in all wisdom; and with gratitude in your hearts sing psalms, hymns, and spiritual songs to God. And whatever you do, in word or deed, do everything in the name of the Lord Jesus, giving thanks to God the Father through him.

—Colossians 3:14–17

TECHNOLOGIES AND THE SPIRIT

"Do everything in the name of the Lord Jesus." Could this apply to our use of our ever-evolving technology and social media? There are a lot of ways to chart the phases of our lives—our pets, schools, children and grandchildren, and jobs. Many baby boomers, like me, also measure our lives in terms of technologies we've used. In college I typed my papers with the manual typewriter I inherited from my mother. I thanked my lucky stars when I was able to purchase a Brother electric typewriter with automatic erasing in graduate school. I purchased my first computer in the mid-1980s and began using the Internet in early 1990s. I started using a cell phone in 2000 when I began to travel extensively. The rest is history with Facebook, Twitter, LinkedIn, GooglePlus, laptops, Kindles, iPads, and iPhones as part of my life and the

life of my family. Once technological wonders, many of these technologies have become virtually mandatory for effective ministerial leadership.

One of my professors, Bernard Loomer, stated that ambiguity ought
to be a theological doctrine. According to Loomer, every advance in the
human adventure brings not only new possibilities but also new compli-
cations and potential dangers. Greater freedom means not only greater
creativity but also the potential for greater destructiveness. Intelligence
can inspire not only adventures of ideas but also diabolical schemes.
The same is surely true of technology. What is intended to simplify life
may complicate our lives. What is created for the purpose of improving
communication may threaten authentic communication. Think of the
following pictures from real life. The other day, as I was enjoying an
afternoon latte and a good book at a local coffeehouse, I observed four
college students sitting at a nearby table; none of them were talking to
their companions, but all of them were texting and checking e-mail.
Lest you think I'm picking on young adults, I was recently involved in a
serious theological conversation with a pastor in his midsixties. Three
times in ten minutes his cell phone rang and he felt compelled to turn
aside to answer it. While I didn't comment at the time, I left the conversation feeling that his phone messages were more important than the
face-to-face pastoral conversation he initiated with me.

Internet, texting, social media, and constant communication have
changed the practice of ministry. But, as the saying goes, "I have good
news and I have bad news." A Unitarian Universalist pastor, Dawn
notes that her smartphone enables her "to be everywhere even if I
never leave home. People can contact me twenty-four/seven and I don't
have to go into the office as much as I used to. I can spend time with my
kids at home and go out to eat and still be in touch if people need me.
The challenge for me is that sometimes I feel people need me all the
time. There's really no boundary between work and home or personal
and private anymore." Bryant, a Progressive Baptist pastor, concurs: "I
can call people hands-free in my car. That's a big deal and saves me a lot
of time, since I spend a couple of hours a day commuting and going
from church to the hospital calls and denominational meetings. But on
the other hand, I don't get much time for quiet. Ten years ago my car
was a place I could be alone; now I'm never alone, and I have to unplug
to have some time to myself." Elizabeth, a Presbyterian pastor, also

recognizes the ambiguities inherent in making technology an important part of her ministry: "Technology, especially social media, has helped with sermon prep. I have access twenty-four/seven to journals, articles, and commentaries and don't need to buy books or go to the library. It has also helped me stay connected with mentors and colleagues, making fellowship, communication, and planning easier. The whole world is at my fingertips. But it has hindered ministry in that some members will e-mail me a prayer request rather than calling or stopping by the church, since they 'don't want to bother me' with what I would not consider a bother at all. And my interest in global issues has often left me feeling overwhelmed and impotent to do anything significant in my rural setting."

Charisse rejoices that she can use technology in congregational worship at her Lutheran parish: "Usually it is an improvement, it enables us to bring art and global music into worship, but when the computer and PowerPoint slides suddenly go down five minutes before worship, sometimes I wish we just went back to paper!" I appreciate her sentiment: today, I did a prerecorded book interview on Skype. I thought it was great, until my host told me the audio didn't pick up, and now we'll have to Skype it all over again. To add to my feelings of ambivalence regarding the Internet, once during an interview with a search committee, the Skype went down, leaving us in the dark for fifteen minutes!

For Melissa, an American Baptist pastor, it's all about connecting and having many portals for communication. She affirms that "technology has enhanced my ministry by making it possible to remain in contact with members who go away to college, both by having virtual contact with them on Facebook and by mailing them care packages we order via the Internet once a year. It has also fostered midweek virtual conversations with church members who spend their work weeks on their computers." She also recognizes that having many portals for communication takes time and can exclude as well as include, especially when Internet use is often age- and income-related. "Dependence on the Internet complicates my ministry because the new forms don't supplant the older methods. It may have once been adequate to announce something in church and put it in the monthly newsletter, but now there are several other methods of communication that need to be used in addition. Everyone has their favorite, so if you don't use every method available, then you aren't communicating with some percentage of the congregation. That's frustrating to them and to me as well." More-over, Melissa notes that initially she assumed that using the Internet for announcements and memos would save paper, but that, in fact, the opposite has occurred. "People send me more messages that they—and I—deem important. I file some away on the computer, but I need others at my fingertips or to take to a meeting, and so my printer is constantly on the go. And because people can jot down a memo or update, they do—and that means I have to read through lots more material on a daily basis from the conference and local ministries than I once did."

Andrew, a Southern Baptist pastor, appreciates the immediacy of the Internet and social media. "It's helped our church become global as well as local. Our members no longer live down the street or around the corner; the days of village ministry are over. But today, at the click of a mouse, we are a global village and a global congregation. We stream services live and later archive them on our website, and that helps members away at school, on holiday, or in the military stay in touch. All this is evangelistic, and that's good news. We can share concerns with folks across the country and newcomers to town. Of course, I miss the hands-on, face-to-face ministry of healing touch. So much of ministry, despite concerns about appropriate boundaries, involves touch—a hug, drying tears, an arm over the shoulder—and I miss that."

My wife, Kate, is a tactile person and deeply involved in healing ministries through laying on of hands and Reiki healing touch. Still, she has found it essential, as a result of geographical distance, to have spiritual direction sessions on Skype. Kate avers, "I prefer it in the room whenever possible, but we can pray and meditate together on Skype and still are able to share God's presence in our lives."

Ministry must keep up with technology and demographics. We are a mobile society and global culture. Once upon a time people were born and died in the same village, and so did their children. That's no longer the case; I am one of many who were born on one coast of the United States and now live on another. I wonder if people initially objected to the apostle Paul's mission to the Gentiles not only because of his hospitality to Gentiles but also because his journeys took him beyond the borders of the Jewish community and its customs.

Still, there are a handful of pastors who prefer the intimacy and pace of an earlier time. Amid the affirmations of technology as necessary for effective ministry, I was surprised to receive a contrasting opinion. A small-town Lutheran pastor in Canada responded, albeit on Facebook, "Some pastors (and their congregations) think they need to be available twenty-four/seven. I don't own a cell phone. The church office and the parsonage have answering machines, so I'm not available twenty-four/ seven, but I'll get the message before too long. My grandfather was a pastor before cell phones or answering machines and he managed very well. I think expectations might have become a little too high, which can't be very good for a 'Healthy Pastor.'" His approach is affirmed by a United Church of Christ pastor, whose congregation is in the Philadel-phia suburbs. Over coffee, he pulled out his ancient five-year-old flip phone and noted, "I don't want to be available twenty-four/seven. All my congregants have smartphones, even the children, and I know that if I had one, I'd be texting, Internet surfing, or responding to texts all day long. Most of them know my cell phone number and in emergencies call me. I don't need to respond to messages about where the coffee urn is or who's teaching the adult class while I'm on a hospital call or leaving a funeral. I am available because I carry my phone and I also have space to contemplate and be present because I don't have all the gadgets. I think that's a good way to do ministry, at least for me."

HEALTHY PRACTICES FOR HEALTHY PASTORS

Technology is intended to be our tool and not our master. Despite the ambiguities inherent in all human achievements, we can use technology in a holy way. Our labor-saving devices can truly save labor and allow us more time for relationships, spiritual practices, and personal and pro-fessional enrichment if we are intentional. Our communication devices can truly bring us together and enhance our personal and professional relationships if we use them prayerfully. (Boundaries are essential to a good life; we need—like Jesus in his retreat in the desert—to say no to certain good things in order to say yes to better possibilities for person-al, professional, and congregational growth) Boundary training, at its best, deals with socially acceptable boundary violations as well as pro-fessional misconduct. The pastor who is available twenty-four/seven and constantly communicating in social media sites, even for the well-being of the church, is violating boundaries of self-care, relational commitments, and professional behavior. If God needs a sabbath to support the creative process and encourage creaturely freedom, then so do today's most dedicated and connected pastors.

Internet Sabbath

Julian is committed to excellence in ministry. He works hard and loves the work of being the pastor of a large, suburban United Church of Christ congregation. Because of his passion for ministry and mission (he is active in issues related to immigration, marriage equality, and sexual trafficking), he has chosen to aim for a fifty-hour week and take specific times away from social media and Internet use. In Julian's words, "I could easily work one hundred hours a week on this job and still feel exhilarated, at least for a while. I love the media and getting to folks on Facebook. I blog about the relationship of social issues to the gospel nearly every day. But, I realize I must address my other passions—my wife, boys, and grandchildren. They keep me centered and balanced. I've come up with a schedule that helps me focus on my family as well as the church and social issues. I turn my cell phone off between Sunday afternoon and midday Monday. My administrative assistant knows to call me in an emergency, and each of my colleagues has an on-call and on-duty day during the week. Otherwise I'm incommunicado. During my sabbath, I put my phone away when I'm with family and don't check the Internet. Monday midday I have lots of messages waiting for me, but it's worth it to be off-line. I've learned that the world can get along without me, and others can pick up the slack at church and in the community."

A Church of the Brethren pastor, Sally feels the same way. She intentionally takes an Internet and phone sabbath every afternoon between three and six to spend time with her children and self-employed husband. "It's our happy hour. We play games and sometimes my husband and I have a glass of wine. For a few hours, we let the world go by. I have caller ID and voice mail, so I listen in to calls, but unless it's a perceived emergency, I wait till after supper."

Another of my former seminary students, Catherine takes intentional minisabbaths from the Internet throughout the week. Her counsel to young pastors like herself is "Remember to turn them off . . . regularly. Remembering God is most important, so it's okay to periodically silence all other voices to seek the still small voice of the Divine. And modeling that is important to our congregants."

Julian, Catherine, and Sally are not legalistic about their sabbath keeping. They are available to amend their schedules in case of a congregational or community emergency. But their intentionality about an Internet sabbath enables them to be present to their families and refreshed for their next pastoral challenge.

Being Present

Spiritual presence is central to fidelity in pastoral care and personal relationships. In that spirit, many pastors also choose to excuse themselves gracefully from conversations when an important call comes in. Spiritual maturity involves always asking the questions, what is my vocation in this particular situation? What is really important here? What is the most fitting thing to do in this situation? If you are anticipating a call regarding a congregant going through a crisis or from a grieving spouse or partner, it is appropriate to check your cell phone or text screen when it rings, but otherwise most calls can wait for the appropriate time. Since the primary tool of ministry is our spiritual attentiveness, we need to consciously place this first in every encounter. Sally states that she "finds inspiration from the theology of Martin Buber. I treat the person in front of me as a Thou. Unless there is an emergency, he or she is the most important person in the world right now, and that means my children as well as a congregant asking a theological question."

A Spirituality of Facebook

I believe Facebook, Twitter, and other social media can be vehicles of spiritual transformation. At the heart of these social media platforms is the belief that the ordinary events of our lives matter. What we do makes a difference to others and to God, and our experiences can be windows into the Divine. While social media discloses plenty of narcissistic rambling and political nitpicking, the spiritual essence of most posts can be summarized by the affirmations:

Our everyday lives are important.
God is in the details of our lives.

Our accomplishments are worth sharing and can benefit others.

I use Facebook and Twitter to share good ideas, reflect on the events of the day, and promote programs and books. I say a prayer of blessing before I post each morning, asking that everyone who reads my posts be blessed. Sometimes I even write a blessing to conclude my posts. I ask that God inspire and be present within my posts to contribute something of value to other people's lives. Often other people's comments call me to pray. I surround them in God's blessing as I pray for health and healing of body, mind, and spirit. I am guided by the psalmist's affirmation, "Let the words of my mouth and the meditation of my heart be acceptable to you, O LORD, my rock and my redeemer" (Ps. 19:14). This affirmation enabled me to respond gracefully, or simply keep my peace, in relation to many otherwise infuriating comments I read on Facebook during the heat of the 2012 U.S. presidential election.

Pray Before Sending

Carrie Newcomer's cute song "Don't Press Send"—this admonition bears repetition—explores the mishaps that occur when someone sends off an e-mail without thinking of its consequences. More than once I have cautioned pastors to pause and pray before sending an e-mail and posting on Facebook. Some things simply can't be taken back in the heat of anger. Moreover, as many pastors have learned the hard way, too much information about last night's party can lead to censure and controversy. The apostle Paul counseled, "Pray without ceasing" (1 Thess. 5:17). I would add my own counsel: "Pray before sending."

As many affirm, social media and the Internet can be the tie that binds and joins people across the nation and the planet. They can connect companions and congregations. I rejoiced to be able to communicate by Skype with my toddler grandson and his family during my Fall 2012 assignment as Visiting Professor of Process Studies at Claremont. In a few minutes, I will be participating in a Skype interview for a congregational theological education program in Scottsdale, Arizona. Many congregations and pastors do search and call interviews on Skype as a way of personalizing the process. I am grateful for social media and the Internet and the gift of global communication that enables me to share good news as a speaker and writer to people across the globe. Like everything else in life, however, our calling as pastors is to use the Internet and social media for the glory of God and the well-being of our brothers and sisters.

5

GLORIFY GOD IN YOUR BODY

Or do you not know that your body is a temple of the Holy Spirit within you, which you have from God, and that you are not your own? For you were bought with a price; therefore glorify God in your body.

—1 Corinthians 6:19–20

LOVING GOD IN THE WORLD OF THE FLESH?

Christian theology has often been ambivalent about the role of embodiment in ministry and spiritual growth. At the heart of our faith as Christians is the incarnation, the word of God made flesh in the life and teachings of Jesus of Nazareth. The incarnation proclaims that the affirmation "God is with us" truly describes God's relationship with humankind and the nonhuman world. Following the wisdom of Genesis and its proclamation of the goodness of life, mind, body, and spirit, Jesus saw whole-person healing as central to his ministry and as a sign of God's coming realm of shalom. Jesus affirmed the intricate interdependence of spirituality, embodiment, and social justice in his ministry of radical hospitality. When Jesus spoke words of affirmation, people's cells as well as souls were transformed. In touching bodies, Jesus transformed people's spiritual identities and transformed their place in society and religious life.

Early Christians described their emerging communities using the image "body of Christ," implying that God's Spirit moved through every member, giving life, light, and guidance. Feeding the poor, healing the sick, welcoming the outcast, and nurturing people's sense of vocation characterized communities that sought to embody God's vision of sha-lom "on earth as it is in heaven." Images of resurrection, while always evocative and mysterious, affirmed the faith that God's love embraces body and spirit in all its fullness, that embodiment shares in God's everlasting life, and that both body and mind are transformed in the loving interdependence of the realm of God.

Still, other Christians viewed the body as a hindrance to spiritual growth. Influenced by Neoplatonic spirituality, many of the parents of Christian theology, including Augustine of Hippo, saw the body as an impediment to spiritual transformation. With embodiment came temp-tation and the lusts of the flesh. Moreover, rather than celebrating sexuality, as Jesus did at the wedding feast at Cana, many early Chris-tian theologians saw sexuality, especially embodied in women's flesh, as a source of temptation and sin. Whereas Jesus and his spiritual parents spoke of the original goodness of creation, the doctrine of original sin served to devalue both sexuality and embodiment. The social justice message of the prophets and the embodied healings of Jesus were mar-ginalized and placed in the background when focus on eternal life be-came the central theme of Christian teaching.[1]

Centuries later, the holistic spirituality of Hebraic and early Chris-tian thought was supplanted by the mind-body dualism of René Des-cartes. Isaac Newton and his followers saw the natural world, including the human body, in mechanistic terms rather than as a revelation of the living God. The immanent, embodied, and incarnate theology of the Hebraic tradition and Jesus's healing ministry was replaced by the machinations of the divine watchmaker, an observer rather than actor in the movements of humanity, nations, and the natural world. No longer were the heavens singing forth the glory of God, nor was our machine-like body revealing God's Spirit with every breath. The body became primarily a transportation device for the mind, an object to be used until it wore out, and not a shrine of the Holy Spirit. The Great Physi-cian whose touch transformed body, mind, spirit, and relationships was relegated to the realm of mythology in favor of a purely body-oriented medicine, for whom spirit, if it existed at all, was a hindrance rather than help in the practice of medicine.

While this brief history of Christianity and embodiment overlooks many of the intricacies of Christian theology and spirituality, I believe it gives witness to three outcomes: a profound turning away from experiencing God's presence in the nonhuman world and our bodies, a neglect of physical embodiment because of an exaggerated focus on eternity, and a devaluation of the relationship of spirit and body in personal and social well-being. I believe that this ambivalence about embodiment is one of the greatest threats to healthy and effective ministry. Reclaiming the "word made flesh" is essential for clergy self-care, healthy boundary keeping, and excellent ministry over the long haul. Our bodies are awesomely and wonderfully made (Ps. 139:14) and should be objects of care and affirmation. They are not machines to be manipulated and worn out but revelations of divine wisdom to be affirmed and cherished.

EMBODIED TRANSFORMATION

You are the temple of God's Spirit. Your body reveals divine wisdom in its intricacy and aim toward wholeness. This is the good news, and the foundation for personal transformation. While this book is health oriented and creation affirming, I recognize the wisdom of Jesus's proclamation, "The time is fulfilled, and the kingdom of God has come near; repent, and believe in the good news." (Mark 1:15). Indeed, God's realm is as near as your immune, circulatory, and cardiovascular systems. The nearness of God's realm challenges us to forsake unhealthy personal and professional habits, repent the harm they have caused ourselves and others, and embark on new pathways of personal and professional healing. We need to explore the ways our lifestyle harms ourselves and others as a prelude to personal and professional transformation.

I was astounded when I ran into Samuel, a Congregationalist pastor. I could barely recognize him. The last time he attended one of my workshops, he weighed more than three hundred pounds, huffing and puffing with every step, filling his plate to the brim, and stepping out for a cigarette break every hour or so. He was a heart attack waiting to happen. But when I saw him a year later, I was amazed at the transformation. He was still on the chubby side, but now he carried his six feet comfortably as he strolled briskly into the meeting room. "What's happened to you?" I asked. "I can hardly believe my eyes. You look great," I marveled, and then I apologized for the boldness of my remarks. In response, Samuel told me of his "come to Jesus" moment: the birth of his first child. An older parent, Samuel was forty when he married and forty-three when his son was born. With tears in his eyes as he held his firstborn, he caught a glimpse of himself in the mirror and that changed everything. "I looked like an old man, and I was just over forty. I wanted to be around to raise my son, but at the rate I was going, I might not make it to his tenth birthday, and that might be a stretch. I decided then and there I needed to change my life. It was a matter of life and death for me and love for my boy." He embarked on a physician-monitored weight reduction program that involved eliminating beef, sodas, desserts, and white flour. He also joined a health club, began an exercise program, including stationary bicycling, the elliptical machine, and weight training. "I feel terrific," he proclaimed. "I have more energy to play with my son, go hiking with my wife, and minister to my congregation. My life is 100 percent better and so is my ministry. How I treat my body is a matter of stewardship, and I want to treat it well. I'm looking forward to coaching his little league team in a few years!"

Sylvia, a Disciples of Christ pastor, described the relationship between her spiritual and physical transformation. She discovered that to truly claim her role as a spiritual leader, she needed to get her physical house in order. In her own words, "As an introvert, the public aspect of ministry was always stressful. I loved the work, but it really wore me down. After preaching two services at my high-demand church, I often came home and took to my bed with a plate of cookies and a soda. Long days at the church, filled with meetings and hospital calls, left me wired. Some nights I binged on ice cream; other nights, I put myself to sleep with three or four glasses of wine. I never got any exercise. I didn't have time, going from dawn to dusk each day. Most of my social activities involved eating or drinking, and after a while my health suffered. My blood pressure and cholesterol skyrocketed. Physically depleted, I finally realized I had to make some big changes." A single, self-reliant person, Sylvia had trouble reaching out at first, but then she realized that the only way she would survive personally, professionally, and physically was to seek help. She sought out a competent spiritual director and also began therapy with a counselor, sensitive to the physical and emotional challenges of spiritual leadership. She also joined a gym and began to work with an athletic trainer. "It's been a long process, getting back into shape, physically and spiritually, but I am becoming a new person. I have a renewed sense of my pastoral ministry, but an equally strong sense of the need to draw boundaries and have a life outside church. I've cut down on my binge eating and late night drinking; I've becoming part of a book group and drama society unrelated to church; and I'm even taking time for coffee dates, and mostly decaf! I attend a 12-step meeting, Overeaters Anonymous. Ministry is sure a lot more fun when it's not the only game in town." Sylvia's blood pressure and cholesterol are in check with medication, and as she gets in better shape, she expects to go off medication entirely in the next year. "It's a miracle," she affirms. "I finally am practicing what I preach and living the faith I affirm, and am learning to care for myself body, mind, and spirit. I don't need to be a martyr for the church. In fact, the healthier I am, the better pastor I am becoming.

I think virtually every pastor has trouble taking care of the temple. I am no exception. While I walk four to six miles daily and meditate at least an hour each day, I've found my belt size increasing as I reach my sixth decade. For me, the challenge is snacking and portion control. So much of ministry and academic life is food related: if they love you, they feed you, and virtually every retreat or program I lead has bountifully laden meals and coffee breaks. Nancy Reagan once said, "Just say no!" I have to say no to myself, eating more lightly and staying away from carbohydrates. I recently took up stationary biking and weight training to achieve greater strength and cardiovascular charge. I still struggle with snacking, especially when I'm writing or preparing talks at my home study. Nothing is more tempting than having a slice of cheese, a cookie, or popcorn for a study break, and I admit, ironically, to this temptation even as I am writing about healthy physical habits. I am working on celery, carrots, and fruit as an alternative. I want to glorify God in every aspect of my life and not just in my preaching, speaking, and writing. I want my physical well-being to be in line with my understanding of God's vision of abundant life, which includes the body as well as the spirit.

TAKING CARE OF THE TEMPLE

Ministerial well-being involves the interplay of theological reflection and spiritual practices. It is grounded in the recognition that the whole earth is filled with God's glory and that everything we do is spiritual in nature. The word and wisdom of God is made flesh in our physical bodies. In fact, we cannot ultimately separate body, mind, and spirit. The body is inspired and the spirit is embodied. Resurrection living implies that God cares about our bodies and that our bodies share in God's vision of everlasting life.

Healthy pastors see spiritual and physical well-being as interdependent. They recognize that exercise and diet can be prayerful in nature. They also see care of their bodies as the most intimate and important area of personal stewardship. As Johanna, an African Methodist Episcopal pastor affirmed, "Embodiment is a gift of God. I can't do ministry, love my spouse, or play with my kids if I neglect my physical well-being. How I treat my body, including the food I eat, taking time for exercise, and getting enough rest, reflects my relationship with God. Neglecting my body is one of the worst forms of ingratitude. I say thank you to God by caring for this wondrous gift, my body in all its fragility and complexity. I want to give God glory everywhere, and that means right here in these flesh and bones. This pastor, like many other healthy pastors, is discovering that three areas crucial to healthy embodiment involve diet, exercise, and rest, all of which are central to blessing our bodies.

During her tenure as a Disciples pastor in Southern California, Adele joined spiritual well-being with physical well-being by walking along the ocean-view path in Laguna Beach. "I would go a mile or two and then find a bench to gaze at the ocean. I'd bring a favorite book to bathe my mind in creativity as I soaked in the beauty of the place. Then I'd walk another mile or two back to the car. I needed this walk on a regular basis to respond to the stresses of a high-demand congregation. Of course, I made sure to wear a hat and put on sunscreen."

BLESSING OUR BODIES

"The world is charged with the grandeur of God," so testifies Jesuit poet Gerard Manley Hopkins. "The whole earth is filled with God's glory," sing the angels during Isaiah's mystical experience in the Jerusalem temple. Wonder, amazement, and gratitude are appropriate spiritual responses to the intricacies of our bodies. They are not primarily hindrances to holiness, temptations to sin, or prisons to be escaped. They are wonders for which to rejoice and be grateful. They reveal God's word and wisdom and call us to faithful stewardship of our own and other people's bodies.

Still, the question rings out: Do you want to be healed? Or, do you want to be healthy? The answer should be obvious, but often our behavior and treatment of our bodies says otherwise. While commitment to a healthy lifestyle does not guarantee perfect health or longevity—we are influenced by environmental, hereditary, and unexpected influences, including accidents of birth, beyond our control—we can make a commitment to love God in the world of the flesh by taking care of the temple we have been given. We can choose to see our care for our bodies as a spiritual practice. Practicing healthy embodiment requires many day-to-day commitments, but most revolve around diet, exercise, and rest.

Sacramental Eating

I recall reading Paul Tillich's comment that we share in the Lord's Supper so that all meals might become holy. Jesus was known in the breaking of the bread, and the early church was characterized by meals shared with glad and generous hearts. Jesus's radical hospitality was reflected in an open table, where everyone had a place, regardless of ethnicity, ritual cleanliness, or gender. Our diets matter: they touch issues of personal stewardship and social and planetary justice.

There is no perfect diet for everyone, but overall well-being is related to diets that join a care for portion control with an emphasis on fruits, vegetables, water, unprocessed foods, and only a modest, if any, consumption of red meat. Health and energy is also connected to the intake of sugar, salt, calories, and fat. An old adage goes, "You are what you eat"; more accurate is, the obvious reality that your energy and vitality reflect what you eat. Healthy diets vary, but as Stephen, a robust Roman Catholic priest, asserts, "Being a priest is a lot like being a cop on the beat. Wherever I go, there are sweet rolls and donuts. I suppose I could eat three donuts and six cups of coffee each morning if I didn't watch out. But when I eat too many carbohydrates or too much sugar, I feel sapped of energy and my mind goes out the window. I have to think of myself as training whenever I write a sermon. On sermon-writing days, I have a light breakfast and only one cup of coffee. I do the same on Sundays when I have three morning masses to celebrate. My diet is 'instant karma' for me. I feel it immediately in terms of energy and inspiration." Jonathan, a Unitarian Universalist pastor, reflects on how giving up sugared soft drinks changed his life: "In the first year, after substituting for water for soft drinks, I lost twenty pounds and ran a half marathon. I also discovered I had more energy for ministry and coming home to play with my two young children."

Steve and Susan, two United Methodist pastors, along with Josiah, a Baptist pastor, connect diet with social justice issues. All three of them have felt convicted by the relationship of red meat to the destruction of the Amazon rain forests. As Josiah stated, "I make sure that when I eat a hamburger, that it's range fed, organic, and raised in an environmentally sound manner. That means that I've cut down on red meat, just because I can't be sure." Steve avers about his coffee consumption, "I've chosen and then convinced my church to use only fair trade coffee. This has saved me money and cut down on my coffee consumption. I want to be able to live justly and this means living intentionally." In college, Susan remembers hearing the words, "Live simply so others can simply live," attributed to Mahatma Gandhi. "These words have changed my life. Eating nonprocessed food as much as possible and being a vegetarian is my way of combining good health with justice to the poor."

Other Christian leaders choose to fast a day a week not only during Lent but also throughout the year, drinking only juices or intentionally skipping a meal once a week, as a sign of solidarity with the poor and as a healthy lifestyle practice. According to Sandy, a midwestern Lutheran pastor, "I need to give my stomach a rest one meal a week. I drink water and juice for lunch on Fridays. I contribute my savings to Bread for the World. This is a justice issue, but it has made a difference in terms of weight and energy," Sandy continued. "I am consciously, albeit vicariously and from a privileged position, in solidarity with the poor. I am also practicing intentionality about what, when, and where I eat, and that's a spiritual issue."

The apostle Paul counsels young Timothy to take little wine for his stomach's sake (1 Tim. 5:23). During the height of the stomach flu season of 2013, I was pleased to see several websites making the connection between drinking a glass of red wine after supper and preventing the stomach flu! And to my joy, that glass of wine did the trick. While there have been no significant studies on the relationship of wine and the flu, red wine has been identified, because of both its content and its stress-reducing properties, with better health. Still, too much of a good thing can be harmful to our health and ministries. Note that Paul says a "little wine," not a symposium with Bacchus! Good health and energy involve not only a balanced diet but also moderate use of alcohol (or none at all if you have substance abuse issues) in tandem with several glasses of water each day. Like all other dietary issues, this is a matter of intentionality and self-awareness. It involves choosing certain behaviors, observing when and where you eat and drink, noting how you feel, and making connections between diet, lifestyle, and justice issues.

Feeling God's Pleasure

One of my favorite films is *Chariots of Fire*. As a study of character and transformation amid challenges of competitive sports, it is a great film for clergy and laypeople alike. One of my favorite lines is Eric Liddell's unapologetic yet humble affirmation, "God made me fast. And when I run I feel his [God's] pleasure." To move with the Spirit is a great joy, yet so many pastors make physical movement a low priority. Julie notes, "I just don't ever seem to make time to exercise. Something always comes up, and my resolutions to walk or go to the gym go out the window." David admits to being a couch potato: "I have plenty of time to exercise, but frankly, it's low on my priorities. I'd rather watch the Patriots or Red Sox play than get out there and exercise. I know I need to, but as the Bible says, 'The spirit is willing but the flesh is weak.' I am wondering these days, however, that maybe my spirit is weak also!"

I recently heard a humorous tale told of a rotund Presbyterian pastor. In itemizing his car mileage for the month, he listed a three-tenths of a mile round trip from the church to the seminary library, which prompted the church treasurer to quip, "If he'd just quit sitting on his assets, he'd be healthier and maybe we could meet our budget!" Said in jest, I wonder if there wasn't more than a little criticism implied. After all, couldn't he muster to walk five minutes down the street to the library?

We are made for movement, even if the biblical account doesn't admonish us to exercise. our parents in the faith didn't have to establish exercise routines: they traveled miles by foot, did hard labor, and rode horses and donkeys! Nevertheless, the temple of the spirit is dynamic and built for action. I realize that exercise is personal, and the type and amount of exercise depends on one's current physical condition and personal preferences. For example, I love to walk and was for many years a cross-country jogger, in part, because I like the outdoors and enjoy the changes that come with each day. Even if I walk the same path daily, as I often do on my predawn, four-mile roundtrip walk to the local Starbucks for coffee and pleasure reading, each step brings a different landscape and something new to see. I find swimming boring and enjoy working out at the gym only if I have a book in hand as I ride a stationary bike. On the other hand, my wife Kate finds walking boring—she thinks I always follow the same route and there's nothing new each day to encounter along the way—and prefers gardening or going to different venues for exercise.

I want to note that before going on any significant new exercise program you need to consult with your health-care provider. You may be able to work up to jogging or elliptical running, but if you haven't been exercising lately, you need to start slowly to avoid exercise-related injuries.

I was pleased in a book on preaching, *Birthing a Sermon*, that one of the authors, Disciples of Christ pastor Barbara Blaisdell, advises preachers to take their sermons out for a walk.[2] That's what I often do in addition to my more structured hour-long morning walk. As part of my practice, I reflect on the lectionary readings for the week and then head out on a midmorning walk, keeping up a good pace, and letting my thoughts move along with my body. I almost always come home with three or four ideas that will guide my sermon writing later in the day. I strongly believe that when your body moves, your mind and emotions are set in motion as well. If you want to experience new ideas, get up off your assets and move!

We are made for motion: our thoughts and bodies move together for health and well-being. A number of holistic health advocates have sug-

gested that, for individuals whose physical condition precludes movement, visualizing themselves in motion enhances their immune system
and reduces stress.

Some pastors, following the example of Eric Liddell, prefer more
dynamic forms of exercise. Sandra experiences the joy of the runner's
high nearly every day as a result of her four-mile run throughout her
suburban neighborhood. "The joy I feel after running carries over
throughout the day. I bring my 'high' to staff meetings, hospital calls,
and sermon writing." One of my good friends, a celibate Roman Catholic priest, saw running as part of his spiritual practice. "I'm a sexual
being, just like everyone else, and I feel the same temptations as every
other man. But when I run I feel truly embodied; my libido goes to
running, and then teaching and preaching, and not to temptation."

Roy, a Central Pennsylvania United Church of Christ pastor, sees
martial arts as a discipline of mind, body, and spirit. He notes that
"martial arts are part of my training for my own individual transformation to become more Christlike. They allow me to become more stress-
free in situations where I deal with death in hospice every week. As you
learn about the body, you also learn how precious it is and also how
vulnerable it can be. The martial arts allow me to develop mind and
body unity, which helps me to think before I act. My Grandmaster's
motto is 'Respect family and friends, maintain good relations with family, no fighting outside or anywhere, train to develop sound mind and
body and learn the art of self-defense, and do all things the right way,
no taking of drugs or anything, which is harmful to my body.' The goal is
to become peaceful with a peaceful mind, never violence." For Roy,
martial arts promote Christlike behavior and enable him to embody the
pathway of Jesus, his model for becoming a "peaceful warrior."[3]

Today many pastors join East and West through the practice of yoga.
Deborah, a West Coast Disciples pastor, notes that her daily practice of
yoga "releases joy and reduces tension and unblocks everything that
keeps me from experiencing the Holy Spirit in my life and ministry."
Sara, a United Church of Christ pastor in upstate New York, sees yoga
as part of her daily meditation. "Yoga positions and breathing center me
and attune me to God's presence in my roles as a parent, friend, and
pastor." Steve practices tai chi movements on a daily basis, after his
morning prayer time. "Tai chi grounds what I've just read in the Daily
Office and brings me both a greater sense of calm and energy to face

the day. Since beginning tai chi, I have more than enough energy for ministry and family life."

As a result of a commitment to joining mind, body, and spirit in holistic forms of exercise, many pastors have experienced "running on plenty at work," to quote United Church of Christ pastor and consultant Suzanne Schmidt.[4] My own energy and focus have increased exponentially as a result of my daily commitment to self-Reiki healing touch. In self-Reiki, I place my hands over the key energy centers of my body and awaken to divine energy flowing in and through them. My treatment always leaves me calm, refreshed, energized, and insightful.[5] Many pastors experience greater energy and well-being through receiving Reiki, acupuncture, or massage treatments. Even the "still touch" of these methods can transform your overall being, and when we move with the Spirit, walking our prayers and praying our breaths, we discover that the whole world is a temple of God's Spirit.

Resting in God

The story of Mary and Martha reflects the two sides of a well-lived personal and professional life. We need to act and also to contemplate. We need not only silence but also stimulation. We need to move forward, and forward movement is often preceded by moving inward in prayer and meditation. As Elizabeth O'Connor of the activist Washington, DC, congregation Church of the Savior asserts, holistic spirituality and spiritual leadership involves the dynamic interplay of the "journey inward" and the "journey outward."[6] How we live the dynamic yin and yang of healthy ministry will depend on personality type (introvert-extrovert), congregational and family situation, and personal gifts. Many sizes fit many people!

The importance of balancing rest and action is essential for healthy ministry, and even for extroverts, in our increasingly market-driven, personality- and performance-oriented, and extroverted culture.[7] The world of social media, Internet communication, and twenty-four/seven availability makes the intentional balance of rest and action central to effective, excellent, and healthy ministry.

Francisco is an off-the-chart extrovert.[8] Constantly on the go from meeting to meeting, both church and civic related, he asserts, "I get my energy off of my relationships with other people. Still, there are times I have to close the door. Enough already! I don't go away for long, but if I take a quick run, then by the time I get back, I'm back on course/ I'm not sure that I could pastor without my commitment to running." Ironically, we need to be more intentional about the rhythm of rest and action during times of crisis and high stress. Jesus rests in the bow of the boat despite—or perhaps because of—the enveloping storm. Out of his deep rest, the Scriptures describe his ability to calm the external storm at sea.

There are many ways to balance rest and action, and inner and external activity. In addition to the obvious spiritual practices I have shared—lectio divina (holy reading), walking prayer, and meditation—I also rest by reading mysteries and watching detective programs on television, most especially the PBS series on Poirot, Sherlock Holmes, Wallander, Midsomer Murders, and Detectives Morse and Lewis. One Saturday after a particularly arduous week of running Lancaster Theological Seminary's Summer Lay and Clergy Academy, I returned home, totally worn out from the week's activities, and then proceeded to watch six hours of the Basil Rathbone Sherlock Holmes movies. After this respite, I was prepared to resume my duties as husband, friend, pastor, and professor.

Laurie, a Southern California United Methodist pastor, describes the need for the right balance of rest and activity in the following way: "A rest is a space between the notes in ministry. It is the place I breathe so that I can keep playing the music of our collaborative work."

Ted and Sharon, two Presbyterian pastors, delight in the flexibility of ministry that allows them to take regular afternoon siestas. Ted extols the virtue of the power nap, "A twenty-minute power nap each afternoon makes all the difference in the world and complements my intentional time of morning meditation." Sharon is thankful that she pastors a congregation of 120 active members whose demands are modest on most weekdays: "I typically take a quick nap every afternoon after a good day at the office and before my two children (eight and six) come home. That way I'm ready for them and for anything that happens at church in the evening." Diane, a Church of the Brethren pastor, believes physical well-being requires mindfulness: "I listen to my body, and when I'm feeling like I'll soon be worn out or a cold is on the horizon, I go home to rest—plenty of tea with lemon and honey, take a zinc tablet and some vitamin C, along with a good book, and a nap—

and by the next day, I'm ready for getting back to the work of ministry."
Diane notes that "I'm not called to be a martyr. If I'm fatigued or sick, I
stay home and don't go to church or make calls unless it's urgent. I'm in
it for the long haul and I don't want to put anybody at risk if I have a
cold or the flu."

Sometimes a variation of typical activities refreshes body, mind, and
spirit. A United Church of Canada pastor, Wanda enjoys making hats
and writing poetry in the bucolic environs of her home. Karen, another
United Church of Canada pastor, finds joy in the company of friends as
a complement to her active but often quite serious ministry: "I use
every opportunity I can to laugh with other people. We go to comedy
clubs, play charades, and go to movie comedies."

HEALTHY PRACTICES FOR HEALTHY PASTORS

I have spent a great deal of time on the issue of embodied ministry
because it is among the most essential yet most neglected aspects of
professional effectiveness and well-being. Virtually all religious traditions include movement among their spiritual practices. Because today's pastors often seek a "two for" in ministry, let me suggest a twofold
approach to walking prayer for the spiritual transformation of preachers. Walking prayer takes many forms: in this first form, you begin
simply with a slow walk in your neighborhood or a pleasant environment. As you walk, breathe gently and slowly, taking note of how you
feel physically, spiritually, and emotionally. You may choose to use an
affirmation such as, "I breathe the Spirit deeply in" as you inhale, and as
you exhale, release any stress or discomfort into God's care. The goal of
this walking prayer is to have no goal except to experience the present
moment as a gift from God.

In the second form, try taking your sermon out for a walk. After
reflecting on the passages for the week ahead in the spirit of lectio
divina, opening to God's wisdom in the words, take a twenty-minute
walk, noticing your environment, how you feel, and any thoughts that
emerge from this week's Scripture readings. Let ideas, images, and
other media bubble up without censorship. After you complete your
walk, take some time to journal insights that come to you on your
walking prayer.

6

LOVING GOD WITH YOUR WHOLE MIND

You shall love the Lord your God with all your heart, and with all
your soul, and with all your mind, and with all your strength.

—Mark 12:30

THE PASTOR AS CONGREGATIONAL THEOLOGIAN

One of my mantras for ministry is "even if the whole theology and
biblical studies departments of the seminary are your congregants, you
(the pastor) are still the congregation's primary theologian." If you are
the senior or solo pastor, week after week you will preach and share
your vision of Scripture, ethics, relationships, spirituality, and theology.
If you're serious about your preaching and study, congregants will come
to you with questions. Most long-term pastors discover that their congregants begin to use phrases and concepts they hear their pastors say
in their sermons.

In many traditions, the rabbinical role of ministry is explicit. The
ordained minister is called to be a teaching elder or pastor and teacher.
Our parents in the faith saw themselves as bringers of good news, pre-
servers of tradition, and interpreters of Scripture. Study was at the heart
of the Protestant Reformation, and the great pastoral voices of Christianity were also teachers and theologians. Take a moment to recall
some of the most significant shapers of Christian theology; virtually all
of them took their role as theologians seriously and essential to their
pastoral task. They saw their ministry as holistic in nature: pastoral care

and spiritual direction shaped their theology and theology shaped their pastoral care. Athanasius, Iranaeus, Augustine, Pelagius, Aquinas, Luther, Calvin, Schleiermacher, Niebuhr, and Barth were, at various times of their lives, working pastors as well as church theologians.

Throughout much of recent history, especially since the Reformation, the pastor was considered among the most educated people in the community. His (and these were primarily men) thoughts were solicited on issues of politics and ethics. A pastor was often among the most—if not one of the few—literate people in the community. While the pastor's status as one of the few intellectual voices in the community has changed radically due to universal education, widespread higher education, specialization, and quantum leaps of knowledge, the pastor still has the responsibility to love God with her or his mind.

Jesus once told a parable about a seed that fell among thorns (Matt. 13:3–7, 18–23). The thorns enveloped the growing plant, literally strangling the life out of it. Jesus compared the growth of this delicate plant to the life of faith: our spiritual vitality can be choked by the cares of the world and, in our time, the many demands of a pastor's life. Sadly, many pastors simply suffer from intellectual laziness or professional weariness. The good news is that transformation is possible for both busy and lazy pastors.

STAYING INTELLECTUALLY FRESH

Two syndromes often plague pastors: burnout and rust out. Burnout occurs when we are confronted by too many emotional and professional demands. Our wellsprings of compassion, creativity, and courage become dry as a result of our pastoral work. We have too much to do and not enough time to do it! Too many crises and not enough time to recover. Too much grief and not enough respite. Too many appointments in our calendar and not enough blank space for refreshment of mind, body, and spirit.

That's how Susie feels. This high-functioning pastor was astonished when she discovered she hadn't read a book in months. She had been on the go pastoring a midsized United Methodist congregation and ministering "day and night," by her own admission. Her ministry embraced not only the spiritual and personal needs of the congregation but also the economic and social needs of the congregation's changing neighborhood and the nation. "I'm building bridges and putting out fires all day long. I get my energy from relationships and problem solving. But it comes at a cost. Reading seems frivolous when there's a homeless family knocking at the door. Sermon preparation goes by the wayside when I'm dealing with a teen facing an unexpected pregnancy or a case of unjustified racial profiling in our neighborhood. On Sunday mornings, I'm barely prepared to preach. I patch together the insights of various online resources, hoping for some sort of theme to emerge. I go home every Sunday, worried that once more I've failed to give my congregants the spiritual nourishment they need. How can I when I don't even study and pray myself?" Extroverted by nature, Susie finds dealing with people's problems exhilarating. Her congregation loves her, but during her last pastoral performance review, the consensus was that her sermons were disorganized, superficial, and hurried. As one who aimed at excellence in her ministry, Susie was both embarrassed and convicted by her congregants' responses.

When Susie and I met for a professional guidance session, she confessed her feelings of intellectual inadequacy and her desire to find an approach to study that worked for her. "In seminary I had to study, although I put my reading off until the last minute if there was a protest or a party. Now it's up to me to find my own rhythm. I don't need to be a professor, but I do need to be an adequate spiritual and theological guide to my congregation."

Susie decided that she couldn't leave her intellectual growth to chance, nor could she wedge it in between the more extroverted tasks of ministry. She decided to get up an hour earlier, before her children and husband awakened, to spend fifteen minutes in prayer and a good forty-five minutes in meditating on the Scriptures for the upcoming Sunday and a few pages of texts I recommended on themes in theology and spirituality. Susie notes that her commitment to study changed her ministry and, unexpectedly, her family life: "Now, my sermons have some real depth and my congregants are telling me that they look forward to hearing me preach. I also realized that I needed to be more intentional about my family life. I can't fit them into the gaps of my heavily booked schedule. I need to place them on the schedule as nonnegotiable. So, except for emergencies and weddings, I block out most of Friday night through Saturday night for family. I'm even finishing my sermons on Friday morning instead of getting up Sunday at 4:00 a.m. to patch something together."

Dave has a different problem. As a small-church pastor who also works as a public school teacher, he admits, "There are just not enough hours in the day to keep up on my studies, and that includes both for class and for church." Realizing he might have only a few hours a week for study and sermon preparation, Dave states that he blocks out an hour after school each day "for reading theology and thinking about my sermon. I also read the Sunday scriptures each morning, doing my own form of ten-minute lectio divina to come up with my own ideas. I'm also a big fan of Textweek, an online resource featuring lectionary commentaries, but I never plagiarize. I want to share my experiences of the scripture, informed by other people's wisdom. I don't want to parrot what others say."

On the other hand, some pastors simply don't take the time or are not challenged to set the bar higher in their sermon preparation and theological preparation. The failure to aim at excellence in preaching often is a sign of too little stimulation and not enough demand in ministry. Excellence in ministry is a dynamic balance of action and rest, grace and challenge, acceptance and demand, and contentment and dissatisfaction. God's grace abounds, but the horizons of spiritual stature are always receding: effective, excellent, and energizing pastors always ask more of themselves than their congregants ask of them. Certain of God's grace, they place high standards on their preaching and pastoral ministry. They know that preaching matters and that what people believe can be a matter of life and death for individuals and the broader culture. As the New Testament demonstrates time and time again, one sermon can transform a person's life and challenge a community to claim a larger mission.

Sometimes pastors rust out as a result of their inability to respond successfully to their congregation's implicit or explicit demands. Having failed time after time to grow their congregations or lead imaginative worship services, they settle for mediocrity. Their grief at failure and at the state of their congregations translates into lowering the bar of adequate ministry and just getting by as preachers and pastors.

More than once I have heard pastors "boast" that they haven't read a theological book or biblical commentary since graduating from seminary. While younger pastors and a growing number of boomers find intellectual stimulation on the Internet, I believe that intentional lack of study is a form of pastoral misconduct. After all, would you go to a physician who told you that he hadn't been to a continuing education program in five years? Would you seek out the services of an attorney or tax preparer who hadn't kept up with the latest legal and tax regulations? Although some people consider the Bible the only book necessary for ministry, I have found that this is typically an excuse for not keeping up with new understanding of biblical passages in light of the challenges of our pluralistic, postmodern age. God is constantly doing a new thing, and so should we. While this may not initially seem like an issue for pastoral self-care, devoting time to creativity, imagination, and study can encourage greater energy and self-affirmation in our ministries and personal lives.

I believe the most effective and excellent pastors take their rabbinical call as seriously as their administrative, pastoral, spiritual, and liturgical roles. Zest in ministry over the long haul is not accidental but the result of a commitment to ongoing spiritual, intellectual, and professional growth. While research on the impact of continuing education or lifelong learning on pastors is only modest, my own anecdotal research through surveys given to pastors participating in Lancaster Theological Seminary's Summer Academy and Clergy Wholeness and Self-Care groups (aimed at pastors at every stage of ministry from first congregational call to preretirement) indicates a strong connection between ongoing study and joy and satisfaction in ministry.

Moreover, according to three studies on the impact of ongoing continuing education on pastors, changes among program participants included "a greater orientation to people and a liberalization of ideas and feelings." Pastors involved in continuing education programs experienced new perspectives on their ministries, a stronger sense of their identity as pastors, and greater awareness of rapid social change.

Three committed and high-functioning pastors shared in conversation the benefits of commitment to intellectual and professional growth in ministry. Each embodied the Jewish affirmation that study is a form of prayer. Loving God with one's mind enhances awareness of God's presence in the world and in the lives of congregants, deepens a sense of connection between the church and the larger society, and encourages new ways of understanding worship, administration, pastoral care, and theology.

Carl, a small town United Church of Christ pastor, holds a DMin. An adjunct professor at a local college, Carl sees study as informing every aspect of his ministry. According to Carl, "it's a drive to understand that thinking about God itself is essential to building up the kingdom of God, and this is a big element of my call as pastor." Carl's scholarly work is reflected in the seriousness with which he takes preaching and in his regular blog on the church's website where he explores new possibilities for looking at ourselves, our vocation, and the world.

Jada, a United Methodist pastor who did her DMin thesis at Wesley Theological Seminary under my direction, states, "I read everything I can, on all sorts of topics. I love to write for pleasure and work. This keeps my mind alert and available to new ideas." Jada says, "I like seeing pastor-theologian as my job description. To me, this calls for an ongoing blend of studying the Scriptures and theology, as well as engaging with people as much as my introversion will allow. I post my sermon exegesis every week on my congregation's website. I teach classes periodically, and I participate in several Bible studies each week." Jada sees her study as a way of nurturing her congregants' ability to think theologically and biblically, and then act politically. She adds, "I really try to stay away from being the Bible Answer Man or Woman (as noted pastor and public theologian Yvette Flunder puts it) and attend to helping people develop the skills and courage to love the Bible and study it critically, and then to put it into practice throughout the week at the office and in community action."

A commitment to ministerial continuing education is a congregational as well as an individual matter. Congregations need to recognize and affirm the connection between professional and intellectual growth through DMin programs, clergy growth groups, continuing education programs, and sabbaticals and a pastor's effectiveness, insightfulness, and happiness in ministry. Pastors can set boundaries to protect their study time, but congregants need to provide financial support and released time to encourage pastoral retreats for theological reflection, Bible study, and professional enrichment. A new pastor in a midwestern United Church of Christ congregation and a former student of mine, Sophia states, "I have a set study day every week that the congregation knows about so they don't expect me in the office or answering a million e-mails. I also attend conferences and insure that I have and use my continuing education time and budget. The continuing education time that I spend away from the church is essential for me and gives new life and depth to everything I do." The quality of these pastors' ministries and intellectual integrity testifies to the fact that pastors should never have to beg for study time from their congregations.

Study is a form of prayer and worship; it enables us to deepen our vocational consciousness and effectiveness in ministry. Spiritual directors share this adage: pray as you can, not as you can't. The same applies to study. Full-time pastors with adequate clerical support and associates in ministry may have more time than bivocational pastors. Introverts may feel more drawn to solitary study, while extroverts may learn best in workshops and study groups. The point is to love God with our mind, recognizing with the author of Psalm 8 that the immensity of the universe calls us to a life of constant spiritual and intellectual growth in our quest to understand our place as pilgrims on a swiftly moving planet, in a solar system, one of a billion solar systems in the Milky Way, which is but one of 125 billion galaxies in our known universe. Awakened to God's grandeur, study inspires us to proclaim "How great thou art" as we assume our vocation as God's partners in healing the earth.

IMAGINATIVE MINISTRY

The Bible is a library of stories of adventurers, pilgrims, and visionaries. If you are looking for the status quo or an unchanging faith, you'd better find another book to read. Holy Scripture invites us to imaginative ministry and living. Abraham and Sarah imagine a new land and then leave their familiar Haran. Moses experiences God in a burning bush and discovers gifts beyond his imagination. Ezekiel sees a Valley of Dry Bones and discovers the breath of God animating the nation's future. Isaiah seeks solace in the temple and discovers God's grandeur and glory illuminate the whole earth; despite his protests of sinfulness, he receives a world-changing vocation. From a young boy's five loaves and two fishes, a multitude is fed, and despite the protests of those who see only death, Jesus revives a twelve-year-old girl. A woman chants the mantra "If I only touch his garment, I will be healed" and is filled with an energy of love that transforms her cells, soul, and social position.

Esther moves from obscurity and passivity to becoming her people's champion.

Pastors had better be imaginative. After all, we daily speak of amazing things—a creative and loving God, a Spirit that gives new life, a baby who transforms human history, and a pentecostal spirit given to all humankind.

Ministry is about thinking big, not living small. It is about a deeper realism that recognizes the limitations of the bottom line, but sees within concrete limitations a world of possibility. Small towns can constrain some pastors, but not Roy. From his vantage point in Central Pennsylvania, he surveys the planet's diversity: "I love to jump into reading religious works from other faiths and nationalities. There is nothing better than worshiping with other nationalities and cultures. Diversity is awesome." Roy loves to pore over the works of the church fathers and reformers, but he is also inspired by process theology and global spirituality. This commitment to seeing life from a large perspective energizes Roy for his ministry to two small-town churches.

Stephanie imbibes possibilities by immersing herself in great literature. An active Presbyterian pastor, she always has a book in hand. "I'm never bored or impatient. If I have to wait at the hospital, for a meeting to begin, or for a tardy congregant, I pick up a book. I always have a few at home on my nightstand and at the church study. I read broadly—I try to read something on the *New York Times* Best Seller list, a recently released novel, and the latest theological texts. I scan the *Christian Century* and Alban Institute's *Congregations* for new perspectives on my work. Books keep me informed but also give me a breadth of thought that comes in handy for preaching and conversations with seekers and congregants."

An active father of three young boys, Santiago doesn't read as regularly as he did in seminary, but he's found a solution—reading Internet blogs on the Huffington Post, Patheos, and Facebook. "I like finding gems and then spending ten minutes reading before one of the boys needs me. I also have found audiobooks helpful when I drive from call to call. I never thought I'd like them—I love the feel of books—but I can't tell you how many books—mysteries, classics, biographies I've listened to as I travel to the hospital or a pastoral call."

The Pastor as Artist

Many pastors are surprised when I remind them that solo or senior pastors typically preach the equivalent of a small book each year. I invite them to see themselves as theological artists who bring together insights from Scripture, literature, and community life for the sake of personal and communal transformation. One of my homiletic mantras is that "if you don't take your sermons seriously, no one else will." I suggest that preachers see their sermons as works of art and spiritual counsel. Even if they preach extemporaneously or without notes, I encourage pastors to write manuscripts and treat their sermons as potentially publishable. This is not an elitist approach to preaching but a challenge to raise expectations about the quality of their sermons.

Many preachers have benefited from creative writing courses, preaching retreats, and texts such as Julia Cameron's *The Artist's Way: A Path to Higher Creativity*, Anne Lamott's *Bird by Bird*, Dan Wakefield's *The Story of Your Life: Writing a Spiritual Autography*, and Natalie Goldberg's *Writing Down the Bones: Freeing the Writer Within*. The pastor as artist of the spiritual imagination will never be bored or boring. Life will present the open-spirited pastor with countless opportunities for theological reflection, spiritual questioning, and ethical challenge.

Growing Edges in Pastoral Study

Imagination enables pastors to grow in wisdom and stature. In living imaginatively, we experience unfolding and ongoing renewal and transformation. A broader, more imaginative approach to life and work liberates us from the constant sense of urgency and the need to solve every problem immediately. A wider perspective enables us to discern the difference between the important, urgent, and unimportant. It gives us a vision to prioritize our ministries in light of our other vocations as parent, friend, family member, citizen, and child of God.

As a result of his participation in one of my pastors' groups at Lancaster Theological Seminary, Tim regularly takes time to ask himself, What new thing is God calling me to do? What adventure is waiting just around the corner? Tim is always looking for possibilities for integrating faithful and forward-looking ministry with his commitment to his wife, young children, and aging parents. Tim acknowledges, "I would be totally overwhelmed apart from the perspective that these times of discernment give me. Along with reading and prayer, thinking about God's calls in my life in ministry helps me to care for my congregation without being enmeshed in it. There is always life beyond the church. I'm better at the church when I am most imaginative in thinking about alternative ways to do ministry, parent, and make a living."

Paradoxically, the more we can look beyond the minutiae of congregational life, the greater our ability to minister to our congregants, explore options for congregational mission, and live by God's vision for us in our time and place.

HEALTHY PRACTICES FOR HEALTHY PASTORS

Romans 12:1–2 has been among the most influential Scriptures in my spiritual development. Not content with a purely disembodied faith, Paul counsels a holistic understanding of mind, body, and spirit. The one in whom "we live and move and have our being" (Acts 17:28) wants us to flourish intellectually as well as physically. In fact, in the yin and yang of ministerial self-care, care for the body and care for the mind enrich, complement, and energize one another. Listen to Paul's words as if they are addressed personally to you. If you took them seriously, in what ways would you change your life? Where do you need whole person renewal? Where do you need transformation so that you might embody the mind of Christ?

> I appeal to you therefore, brothers and sisters, by the mercies of God, to present your bodies as a living sacrifice, holy and acceptable to God, which is your spiritual worship. Do not be conformed to this world, but be transformed by the renewing of your minds, so that you may discern what is the will of God—what is good and acceptable and perfect.

Many of you who know my work will remember how the use of spiritual affirmations has transformed my life, marriage, writing, and ministry. My wife and I used regular affirmations to save and transform our marriage some thirty years ago, and I still use affirmations as a way of awakening to Christ within me, the hope of glorious things to come.

Affirmations are simply positive statements, said in the present tense, to awaken our whole being to the deeper realities of our lives and God's abundant life as it energizes and enlivens us. As a writer of books, articles, blogs, and sermons, I say the following words as I retire each night: "While I am resting, great ideas are coming to me and I will write them down tomorrow." While I can't attribute all my writing—both inspirational and mediocre—to the use of affirmations, I must confess that I have never had writer's block. This may be partly due to another affirmation I regularly use before retiring each evening: "Creative insights constantly come to me and I express them in life-changing ways." In Philippians, Paul sees affirmations as essential to Christian spirituality:

> Finally, beloved, whatever is true, whatever is honorable, whatever is just, whatever is pure, whatever is pleasing, whatever is commendable, if there is any excellence and if there is anything worthy of praise, think about these things.
> —Philippians 4:8

Paul is suggesting that the images we focus on can produce health or illness in our lives. They open us to new possibilities or trap us in the prisons of the past. Following this counsel, Paul presents Christian soul food at its best:

> I can do all things through [Christ] who strengthens me.
> —Philippians 4:13

> And my God will fully satisfy every need of yours according to his riches in glory in Christ Jesus.
> —Philippians 4:19

In my practice of affirmative spirituality, I regularly repeat affirmations throughout the day to keep my eyes on Jesus and awaken me to God's energy of loving creativity that supports every moment of life. In that spirit, take some time to repeat some of the following scripturally based affirmations, or create affirmations that suit your particular life situation.

Nothing can separate me from the love of God.
I am created in God's image.

I am God's beloved child.

I am the light of the world.

God's light shines in and through me to bring light to others.

The good work God has begun in my life, God will bring to fullness, and it will be a harvest of righteousness.

In all things, I am a [peaceful conqueror] through God's presence in my life.

I have also personalized affirmations to fit particular situations in my life. Some of my favorites are these:

Good ideas are constantly coming to me, and I share them insightfully.

I give Christ to and receive Christ from everyone I meet.

I see Christ in everyone I meet.

God's wisdom guides my every step.

I bless everyone I meet.

I am an insightful preacher and speaker.

As you listen to your own life, what spiritual affirmations would deepen your relationships and ministry? What words of faith will open your heart and mind to embrace God's possibilities for your life?

Busy pastors, especially those with children, may find my suggestions unrealistic given the many demands on their time. I honor their busyness—I have been an active parent and pastor too. But the issue is not doing one more thing; rather, the issue is the way we practice ministry and taking a careful look at how we spend our time as parents, partners, and pastors. We can pray our way through busy days and expand our minds while listening to audiobooks as we drive to pastoral appointments.

7

HAVING THE TIME OF YOUR LIFE: MAKING FRIENDS WITH TIME IN MINISTRY

Stress will kill you as fast as a bullet. Find your peace and live there.

For everything there is a season, and a time for every matter under heaven:

> a time to be born, and a time to die;
> a time to plant, and a time to pluck up what is planted;
> a time to kill, and a time to heal;
> a time to break down, and a time to build up;
> a time to weep, and a time to laugh;
> a time to mourn, and a time to dance;
> a time to throw away stones, and a time to gather stones together;
> a time to embrace, and a time to refrain from embracing;
> a time to seek, and a time to lose;
> a time to keep, and a time to throw away;
> a time to tear, and a time to sew;
> a time to keep silence, and a time to speak;
> a time to love, and a time to hate;
> a time for war, and a time for peace.

—Ecclesiastes 3:1–8

Dirty Dancing

THE TIME OF YOUR LIFE

Time is a profoundly theological issue. It reflects our understanding of God, the creative process, history, human life, and our values as God's companions in ministry. One of my favorite reflections on the nature of time comes from the pen of Henry van Dyke, pastor, professor, lyricist who is known for the words of "Joyful, Joyful, We Adore Thee," and author of "The Other Wiseman," my favorite Christmas story, read first to me on my Baptist pastor father's lap: "Time is too slow for those who wait, too swift for those who fear, too long for those who grieve, too short for those who rejoice, but for those who love, time is eternity."

Time is, as Plato asserts, "the moving image of eternity" for those who believe in a wise, active, and intentional God. We can chart time in terms of moments, hours, and days. With some pastors, we can ponder the question, how will we spend the 168 hours allotted to us each week? Or in the words of the "Seasons of Love" from the musical *Rent*, we can meditate on what values we will embody in the 525,600 minutes given to each of us every year.

Many people attempt to manage time, but I believe time is ultimately unmanageable; it is often chaotic, novel, and emerging, and it is always beyond our grasp. That's what makes our lives as pastors both interesting and challenging. As one pastor noted with a sense of wonder, "A knock on my door can turn my day upside down and a phone call can turn a week of anticipated and leisurely study into a maelstrom of funeral planning and grief counseling." We cannot manage time, but we can be intentional about how we spend the time of our lives. We can live by a vision or mission that enables us to respond gracefully, creatively, and calmly even in the most challenging and action-packed weeks.

For those who love their friends, families, and congregants and who experience God in the finitude and perpetually perishing nature of life, there is always enough time . . . for ministry, for family, for love, and for study. It's a matter of joining healthy theology with self-awareness as we go about our personal and professional lives. Our times are in God's hands; and in the everlasting interdependence of life, we are always on holy ground, sharing in God's abundant life that joins us with all creation, from the big bang to the unimaginable future God envisages for the universe.

Still, pastors can be imprisoned by the tyranny of the urgent. Like the White Rabbit from Alice's *Adventures in Wonderland*, we can scurry about, muttering under our breath, "I'm late, I'm late, for a very important date," with little or no vision to guide our footsteps. Take, for example, Lucy, a single pastor of a Lutheran (ELCA) congregation in Minnesota: "Sometimes I feel like I'm chasing my tail. Or maybe I really am chasing my tale. I have so much to do and so little time. I feel hurried as I go from appointment to appointment and task to task. I've heard that nature abhors a vacuum, but I'm beginning to think this is also true of ministry. The minute I get some me time, the phone rings and I'm off and running. I need to press the pause button in my tale of ministry and relax awhile, knowing I don't have to be in control or know everything's that's going on to be a faithful and effective pastor." Sandra, also a single, female pastor, laments, "So many things, jobs, people take longer than estimated. Then I run late and leave a bad impression. I put people first, even above my own well-being, and their needs seem never to end. As a single, female pastor I have to leave town to have personal time."

Lest you think that time issues affect only women, Tom, a bivocational Disciples of Christ pastor, finds his daily shift from high school teaching to pastoral care, sermon preparation, and church business often jarring: "Sometimes I ask myself, Where am I? and What am I doing? I feel a disconnection between my day job and my off-hours ministry, and experience a lot of stress on weeks when I'm trying to juggle a few hospital calls and a funeral with my teaching assignments. I feel like I get lost in the middle of all this. I love to teach and need the income, since my church can afford only a part-time pastor, and I love ministry, but sometimes it's just too much! God grant me an extra hour a day! Maybe, I'd catch up."

Physician Larry Dossey has coined the term hurry sickness to describe our attitudes toward time. We try to juggle activities with the kids, multitask, and cultivate a prayer life and are never really present to this glorious moment of time. In the spirit of the words from Ecclesiastes above, take a moment to reflect on your attitude toward time: Is time spacious and abundant? Or do you feel rushed, always hurrying and never seeming to catch up? Is time a blessing or a curse? When you think of time, do you feel calm or anxious? Is your attitude toward time a factor in your overall well-being? While it is clear that we can't control the external events of our lives, perhaps we can change our attitudes toward time and find health rather than illness in the time of our lives.

In reflecting on his own experience of time, George shared the following comments that mirror the experiences of pastors of every age, marital status, and denomination. "Time feels scarce because as a pastor you often get caught up in the busy work of church life. What I mean by busy work for pastors is the things that just have to get done—too many hospital and senior center and shut-in visits, denominational meetings, administrative reports and other time-consuming actions—that don't really move the congregation in a direction either of deeper relationships with Christ for themselves or of encouraging or leading others to Christ through evangelism and modeling. I guess I was a dreamer when I graduated from seminary. I really expected to bring churches to new heights in mission and ministry, to get them to move and change. . . . I think time too often becomes a measurement of things not accomplished, and that's what leads to burnout."

In many respects, time is all we have to be faithful, to bring beauty to life, to love, and to respond to the challenges of pastoring in Christ's place. As the Hebraic understanding of sabbath makes clear, all time is holy, whether or not we are aware of it. In the midst of a busy schedule, God meets us each moment; and each moment, if we are attentive, shares in God's everlasting life. Abundant life is ours and we always have enough time for ministry.

THE SANCTUARY OF TIME

One of my favorite songs is "Holy as a Day Is Spent," penned by Carrie Newcomer.[2] This hymn of practical mysticism celebrates what author Kathleen Norris describes as the "quotidian mysteries" of life: doing dishes, observing a dog running in her sleep, passing time with a check-out clerk, folding laundry, writing a poem, and watching geese fly overhead. These are all a part of God's gentle providence, which awakens us to the sacrament of this present moment. If you are a pastor, this same holiness can be experienced in working on the church newsletter, driving to a denominational meeting, seeing a child run up the aisle for the children's sermon, preparing a sermon, or holding hands with a senior adult at the nursing home.

Tea-bag wisdom transformed Sharon's understanding of time. While enjoying a good cup of afternoon tea, Sharon noticed a message on the tag affixed to the tea bag: "When God created time, God made enough of it." She avers, "That really convicted me. It's not just about me. I'm part of a bigger story. My little story of busy ministry fits into God's creation of the universe and God's story of salvation among the Hebrews, Jesus's ministry, and the early church. When I remember that I'm part of this grand story, time stretches out, and even on a busy day I can take a moment to breathe deeply the spacious presence of God." Lauren, a United Church of Christ pastor and former student of mine, affirms, "Time—there is never enough, but when I pause and receive a hug from Jesus, take a deep breath, then I find there is usually enough time for the ministry and life and all other important things, like alone time, relaxation, fun, love, family, friends, others, pets, home. If I do this, I can accomplish pastoral care matters better."

Roy, a pastor of a two-point charge, sees time as Spirit filled. In contrast to some pastors, he doesn't try to manage time; instead, he goes with the movements of God's Spirit, letting the winds of the Spirit guide him throughout the day. He admits, "I never make a schedule. I find that the Spirit drives my day. However, I also have good congregations that don't require me to follow an eight-to-five schedule to be effective. They also recognize that I need rest in order to do my best work as their pastor." While not everyone—especially Myers-Briggs "judging" types like myself who thrive on making lists and having schedules—feels comfortable embracing Roy's extemporaneous approach, Roy's "perceiving" approach to ministry is deeply intentional: it reflects Jesus's vision of the Holy Spirit, "The wind blows where it chooses, and you hear the sound of it, but you do not know where it comes from or where it goes. So it is with everyone who is born of the Spirit" (John 3:8).

Although I begin each day with a clear vision, I do not follow a strict agenda for each day's unfolding. I have learned to treat my daily and weekly schedules as I do the Bible and the U.S. Constitution; that is, to treasure the words and also hold them loosely and flexibly, recognizing that context is everything in life and ministry. While we may cherish a long-haul vision that guides our lives and sets our priorities, we must always remember that God has a vision, albeit flexible and open to our input, for each moment and for the long haul, and that each moment of life has its own vocation.

STRATEGIES FOR MAKING TIME YOUR FRIEND

Everybody has same number of hours in a week and minutes in a year. How we approach the time of our lives makes the difference between health and illness, excellence and mediocrity, zest and boredom, and abundance and scarcity. Our approach to time is profoundly contextual. We navigate the days of our lives in relationship to a variety of factors: our marital status, pastoral responsibilities and congregational size, conditions of employment, family life, age, and personal gifts.

A growing number of baby boomers, like my wife and me, are members of the sandwich generation. We divide our relational responsibilities between growing children—and grandchildren—and aging parents. Sometimes the emotional demands of parenting and grandparenting or being the primary caregiver of an aging parent take up virtually all our emotional energy. We are so depleted from hospital visits, daycare arrangements, and trips to the doctor, soccer practice, and music lessons that we have little emotional attention to give to our congregants or our spouses. But being sandwiched means we have to be all the more intentional about balancing our time and keeping our emotional and spiritual wellsprings fresh and vital.

Kathy, a single parent of two and pastor of a struggling town and country Presbyterian church, often just tries to get through the day. Every morning she receives a call from her physically challenged mother who recently relocated to an apartment in a community five miles away. Her ex-husband, now remarried, lives in a midsized city two hours away. That means day-to-day care of her children—and her mother—is on Kathy's shoulders. "It's nonstop some days. I try to get up an hour early for prayer and exercise. Once I drop the kids (ages eight and eleven) at school, I head out for church and calls until about 3:00 p.m. A few times a week I bring my mom over to the house for supper; and the boys usually attend night meetings and play in a classroom adjoining the church boardroom." Kathy admits that the rhythm of her life is challenging, but her saving grace has been the weekends when the boys are away. "I love my boys. But I breathe a sigh of relief when my ex-husband picks them up, usually two to three weekends each month. I miss the noise and companionship, but I try to claim Friday evening to Sunday evening, minus church activities, as time for study, prayer, and friends. On Fridays, I go out with a few of my clergy friends, usually for an inexpensive dinner and a movie. Saturday, after I straighten up the house, I read, exercise, and pray. It restores my soul to bathe myself in quiet. My mother goes to church with me on Sunday and usually comes over to lunch while I do the laundry. I take us both shopping for the week ahead and then come home and read some fiction. I love mysteries, and usually take a nap until the thundering herd returns. My commitment to friendships and time to myself help me reduce the stress and hurry of ministry and give me a sense of 'enough' when it comes to balancing the demands of family and ministry."

Steve takes his time away from church life seriously. In describing his approach to ministry, Steve states, "I am very intentional about taking time off from church. Sometimes I just head out for a half-hour walk in the middle of the day. Other times I find a babysitter and take my wife out for dinner and a movie. I take an afternoon off just for myself. Even though I'm an extrovert and could give a TED talk at the drop of the hat, I know it's easy for me to skate by on my persona and preaching style when I need to address issues with sensitivity and depth. On my afternoon off, I usually jog three miles to my favorite coffee shop with a few books or Kindle in my backpack, and then immerse myself in a book. I try to do this twice a week; on Mondays to really get to know the lectionary readings and on Thursdays to deepen my study. I typically write my sermon on Friday morning."

Many younger pastors, especially from generation X, no longer feel the need to spend forty hours a week in the church office. When a patriarch of her church noted that he spent more time at church than she did, Carol responded, "My calling is to be on the move and not stand still. With a cell phone and texting, I can pastor anywhere. If I stayed put in the church building, this church would die." Carol, like many younger pastors and some of their elder brothers and sisters, "go into the world" and spend much of their time meeting congregants and potential members in coffee shops and restaurants. Carol notes that she takes advantage of the flexibility of her schedule. In the course of the day, she moves seamlessly and prayerfully from mom and partner to pastor, building manager, and CEO, and then back home to be mom and partner and to make a few final calls and reflect on the upcoming sermon.

A member of one of Lancaster Theological Seminary's pastoral spiritual formation groups, Carol has taken seriously my mantra about time and ministry: "Most of a pastor's week is discretionary. After you've shown up for the essentials—preaching, worship, staff supervision, and committee meetings—how you spend the rest of the week is up to you. If you work out a flexible and agreeable schedule with your congregation, you can choose a ministerial style that suits your personality, work style, family and marital situation, and personal goals."

Still, even with the flexibility built into ministry, pastors need to be intentional about the hours they regularly work each week. Scores of pastors have noted some variation on the following statement from Young, a Presbyterian pastor: "I have a lot of free time, but I'm never sure when I'm off the job. I may get a great idea for a sermon or a church program in the middle of my morning walk. I get text messages at all hours and feel like I need to respond quickly. I have to be very intentional to clock out and really be off." Another Presbyterian pastor, Rosandra, asserts that she makes a practice to say to herself, "I'm done when I come home for good in the late afternoon or early evening." A neat freak, Toby describes ministry as being like "housework, in that it's never really done, nor can it be done. Because I know that not taking a day off is bad both for my emotional and physical health, I force myself to take a day off. I tell my church I will take messages at 8:00 a.m. and 4:30 p.m., and that I will check my messages in the midafternoon. If it's a matter of life and death, I've asked them to call the chair of the board who will relay messages to me."

Karen, a part-time United Church of Canada pastor, keeps good track of her weekly schedule. "I'm contracted to work only three-quarters time, and that means thirty to thirty-five hours a week. If there are emergencies and I have to work overtime, I arrange with the church council to compensate for that time during one of the following weeks." Things get pretty dicey for part-time pastors when tragedies force them to work overtime for several weeks in a row. Karen recalls "having four deaths, including a young mother killed in a car accident, over a three-week period. Because my church is one of three congregations in our town, I serve as a type of chaplain to the whole town. I have to respond to crises even if the person in crisis has never darkened the door of a church. It took some negotiating, but the church council arranged for a retired pastor to cover for me so I could take a whole week off, Sunday after church till the next Monday. I came back rested and ready."

Even full-time pastors have to keep track of their hours. Studies indicate that if pastors work consistently more than fifty or fifty-five hours a week, they become candidates for stress-related illness, emotional fatigue, and physical exhaustion. Vera notes that she "always keeps track of her hours. I'm very flexible with how and where I work, but keeping track of my hours is like taking my temperature, checking my blood pressure, or getting on the scale; it serves as a barometer for my overall well-being in ministry. You always have to finish the job and do it well, and that may mean long hours some days and weeks, but when the weeks are light, I take advantage of them by taking an extra day off, coming home early, and getting ahead on my sermons and professional reading."

A dynamic that is changing the shape of ministry is the growing number of single ministers in their twenties and in midlife. Single pastors often feel that congregations expect them to work more hours because they don't have intimate family ties. Thirty-year-old Theresa, a pastor of a county-seat Lutheran church, speaks for many single pastors when she states that "I have to educate my congregation to respect my time as much as they would a married person. It's true that I don't have children to feed and get off to school each morning or a husband with whom I must take time for dates and shared responsibilities. But, I do have a life—and sometimes I have to drive two hours to meet friends for lunch or a night out. I'm on my own and that takes time!"

While pastors employ many healthy strategies in balancing the many responsibilities of personal and professional life, the one thing they all have in common is intentionality and self-awareness. They have a vision of ministry, worked out flexibly in daily life, that guides their daily and weekly decision making and prioritizing. They also practice self-awareness, observing their overall sense of physical, emotional, and spiritual well-being and making adjustments when they begin to feel hurried, stressed, off-kilter, or emotionally drained.

TRANSFORMING SABBATH

Sabbath is at the heart of the Jewish-Christian spiritual vision. The creative process requires an ongoing rotation of action and contemplation. Even God rests to make room for human creativity. According to the first creation story (Gen. 1:1–2:4), in God's creative unfolding of the universe, God affirmed the world as "good" and then

> God finished the work that he had done, and he rested on the seventh day from all the work that he had done. So God blessed the seventh day and hallowed it, because on it God rested from all the work that he had done in creation.
>
> —Genesis 2:2–3

God's own willingness to rest, trusting the universe and ourselves to be partners in creation, is the model for our own professional practices:

> Remember the sabbath day, and keep it holy. Six days you shall labor and do all your work. But the seventh day is a sabbath to the LORD your God; you shall not do any work—you, your son or your daughter, your male or female slave, your livestock, or the alien resident in your towns. For in six days the LORD made heaven and earth, the sea, and all that is in them, but rested the seventh day; therefore the LORD blessed the sabbath day and consecrated it.
>
> —Exodus 20:8–11

Isaac Luria (1534–72), one of the parents of Kabbalah spirituality, spoke of divine creativity in terms of the dynamic relationship of activity and repose. Tzimtzum describes God's making space for human creativity by taking time for retreat or withdrawal. Following God's example, healthy ministry involves regular times of retreat and withdrawal. In resting from our professional labors, we enable our congregants and colleagues to develop their own skills in effective and inspiring ministry. Healthy ministry involves taking intentional times for rest and relaxation. More than just recreation, sabbath time is also intended to reconnect us with God's ubiquitous grace. Sabbath is a profound act of trust in God's faithful care of creation and us. We let go of perpetual doing, trusting that God and others will sustain us and the institutions we love during our times of rest and replenishment. As Abraham Joshua Heschel proclaims, sabbath is the sanctuary of time, connecting us with the ground of all becoming and blessing us with wisdom and energy.

Jesus once proclaimed, "I am the vine, you are the branches" (John 15:5). When we are connected with God, we bear fruit. Disconnected from the divine source of energy, we wither and our ministries lose their zest. Emotional burnout is just around the corner.

In their quest for spiritual wholeness, some pastors are able to make a commitment to practicing an authentic sabbath. Sarah practices a weekly sabbath, except when congregational emergencies intrude on her spiritual disciplines. Given the nature of her ministry and family, her sabbath extends from Sunday afternoon to Monday afternoon. Sunday afternoon is family time. After decompressing from morning worship, Sarah and her family (her partner and their two children, ages seven and five) have a traditional, midafternoon Sunday supper, followed by games or a movie and then baths and bed. Monday after the children have left for school and her partner has gone to work, Sarah takes a "quiet day" for prayer, journaling, study, and reading. Her administrative assistant and church leaders contact her only in case of an emergency. Sabbath ends on Monday night with dinner and time with her partner and the kids. According to Sarah, "Sabbath has transformed my ministry and sense of time. Sabbath slows down time and gives me depth in ministry that I never had before. I have come to see prayer, meditation, and study as interdependent in my personal and professional life. My sermons are more alive now, and the week ahead feels more spacious, even on busy weeks."

Many pastors, because of the nature of their ministries and family involvements, have learned to transform time through minisabbaths. A bivocational pastor patching together church, home-care nursing, and family, Thad has virtually no time for a traditional sabbath. His automobile has become his "mobile sabbath." "As I go from one medical appointment to the next, I listen to Christian music and pray at every stoplight. On my way from the car to my home visits, I breathe deeply and pray to be a messenger of God." The few hours that Thad spends at the church office have become a "spiritual sanctuary." Because few people stop by his small-town congregation of seventy-five members, most of his time at the church is spent in prayer and study. According to Thad, "I make it a point to take a few minutes for prayer after arriving at church; and on Sunday mornings, I come early and circle the sanctu-

ary with prayer. I could never do a whole-day sabbath, but short times
of prayer make all the difference in my ministry and family life."

A card-carrying member of the sandwich generation, Jody sees sabbath as a form of "preventive medicine and spirituality." Jody reports, "I
feel torn between the responsibilities of parenting, of marriage, and of
regular care for two sets of aging parents and the needs of the church.
But every Friday afternoon I go away to a quiet place, a local monastery, for prayer, meditation, and walking. My afternoon begins with a
silent meal. Then I retreat to either the monastery library or the gar-
dens, depending on the weather, for quiet prayer and reading something in theology or spirituality. I love walking the grounds, bathing my
senses in the beauty of the place. As Psalm 23 says, these Friday sabbath times 'restore my soul' and prepare me for ministry."

SACRED TIME, SACRED SPACE

A flesh-and-bones God comes to us in time and space. Relativity physics
reminds us that time and space are dynamically interdependent. Although the whole universe, as the philosopher Alfred North Whitehead
states, conspires to create each moment of experience, every moment is
concretely grounded in a particular communal and geographical context. Spirituality is never abstract but always contextual, emerging here
and now in this place and time.

Time and space can become windows into the Divine. Theologians
speak of kairos and chronos time. Chronos time is clock time, the even
flowing of seconds, minutes, hours, and days. Within chronos time,
unique and transformative moments emerge. Kairos time is transformational and incarnational; God meets us in the movement of the clock.
We can experience everlasting life in the perpetual whitewater of twenty-first-century professional life.

Sacred space can also become the portal through which we experience God's companionship. As a student of Celtic spirituality, I am
enamored of the Celtic notion of thin places. Thin places join the everlasting and the passing and the sacred and secular. The story of Jacob
and the ladder of angels describes one such thin place: after awakening
from a vivid dream, Jacob exclaims, "God was in this place and I did not
know it." In encountering a thin place amid the busyness of our minis-

tries and domestic lives, we discover God is in this place; that is, every place and every encounter.

The transformation of time invites us to see time and space as icons of divine artistry and companionship. In working with pastors, I often ask the following questions: Where is your sacred space? What is your holy time? If they are unable to answer, I invite them to consider: What places in your daily life might become sacred to you? What times of day are most transparent to God's presence and inspiring of prayer and meditation? An omnipresent God can be experienced anywhere and anytime, but we need to pause long enough to experience God's revelation in the daily events of life and ministry.

In the course of writing this book, my sacred space was my high-rise Chevy Chase, Maryland, study. My leather arts and crafts recliner was my venue for writing, thinking, praying, and meditating. My sacred time that illumines every other time of the day is predawn. As I noted earlier, I wake up around 5:00 a.m., meditate and study, and then head out for an hour-long walk. When I return home, I'm well prepared spiritually and physically for whatever novelties the day will bring. Now that I live on Cape Cod, most mornings involve an hour's walk along the Nantucket Sound with waves and seagulls for company.

Kevin's sacred place is his congregation's study, where he truly prays and reads. Kevin notes that in the afternoon after the administrative assistant has gone home, "my study becomes a sacred space and the afternoon becomes my sacred time in which I pray, read, journal, and write." Inspired by his regular spiritual practices of quiet prayer and meditation, Kevin delights in writing sermons, blogs, and occasional devotional pieces for denominational publications. "Those ninety minutes, four times a week, connect me with God and my sense of vocation. I come away inspired and energized for the rest of my ministry."

Maria's sacred space-time is her sunroom and adjoining garden. "I delight in the sun shining into my simply furnished solarium, warming me as do my daily sung prayers and devotions. When the weather is clement, I go out into the garden and discover God in soil and sunshine. I like the messy spirituality of humus and getting my hands dirty digging, cutting, and potting."

Time and space become windows into revelation when we awaken to God's omnipresent movements in our lives. God is right here as you read this text, inspiring, energizing, challenging, and providing possibilities for faithful ministry and loving relationships. Regardless of your life situation, there is still time, perhaps even a few moments, to embrace God's quiet nearness and let that illumine the rest of the day.

HEALTHY PRACTICES FOR HEALTHY PASTORS

It has been said that being a pastor is like being a dog at a whistler's convention! Amid the numerous, and often conflicting, demands on our time and energy, pastors need to find a still point, a sacred space-time, that binds these many tasks into an intricate fabric of pastoral wholeness. In embracing the holiness of each moment, we can experience God's pleasure within the quotidian tasks of pastoral ministry.

For everything there is a season, and—according to Ecclesiastes—divine wisdom shapes the contrasting seasons of life. Within the mysteries of time and space, God seeks wholeness of mind, body, and spirit. God wants us to enjoy the time of our lives. Spiritual practices are intended to bring joy to our personal and professional lives.

> What gain have the workers from their toil? I have seen the business that God has given to everyone to be busy with. He has made everything suitable for its time; moreover he has put a sense of past and future into their minds, yet they cannot find out what God has done from the beginning to the end. I know that there is nothing better for them than to be happy and enjoy themselves as long as they live; moreover, it is God's gift that all should eat and drink and take pleasure in all their toil.
>
> —Ecclesiastes 3:9–13

Breathing the Tasks of Ministry

Without breath, there is no life. The quality of our breath often reveals our current state of mind and well-being. A practice that has transformed my life as a pastor, teacher, and writer involves taking a breath every time I move from one task to another. When I enter my study, I take a deep breath, opening to God's centering and healing energy. When I log on to the computer, I take another deep breath, opening to that same divine inspiration and insight. When the phone rings, I say a prayer as I breathe in God's relational presence. When I sign on to

Facebook or Twitter, I breathe God's presence and openness to divine inspiration in those with whom I will communicate and those who will read my posts. Breathing the many tasks of ministry creates a fabric of relatedness in which all the events of our lives become components of a lively tapestry of wholeness.

Moving in Time

Many people pin their theologies on the success of their parking-lot prayers. They believe that one of the clearest proofs of God's existence is getting the parking place closest to their destination. At the risk of being a contrarian, I want to suggest an alternative for pastoral wellness: when you're making calls, whether of congregants, at the hospital, or over a cup of coffee at a restaurant, park as far away as reasonable and possible. The extra steps will burn calories, calm any stressful feelings from the drive, provide an opportunity for reflection, and transform the experience of time. In addition to parking a reasonable distance away from your destination, I suggest taking a few moments for short prayer and centering breath prior to entering a hospital room, congregant's home, or coffeehouse. If weather permits, I walk to most appointments within thirty minutes of my home or study. Gentle movement reduces stress and anxiety and is one of the most effective antidotes for feelings of busyness.

Listening to Your Body

Hurry or time sickness often registers itself in our physical condition. Pause awhile not only to experience the beauty all around you but also to get to know your body. Psalm 139 proclaims we are awesomely and wonderfully created. Accordingly, you can meditate on your embodiment, as a variation of the traditional practice of examen, or "examination of conscience." How do you feel today? Are you energized or fatigued? Are you feeling stressed or calm? Where do you register stress and fatigue? How are feelings of busyness reflected in your physical well-being?

"The heavens declare the glories of God" and so do our nervous, cardiovascular, digestive, and immune systems. When you listen closely to your body, you can learn practices and attitudes that promote health and healing. That's what incarnation is about, loving God in the world of the flesh and seeing your body as a reflection of God's wisdom.

Looking at the Time of Your Life

This chapter began with the assertion that one thing every person has in common is a 168-hour week. While flexibility is essential to any spiritual practice, looking at how we spend the time of our lives is the first step to transforming our sense of time. As an examination of conscience, consider the following questions:

What does your typical day look like?

In what ways do your values shape your decisions throughout the course of a week?

What percentage of your day or week do you spend on pastoral calls, study, sermon writing, administration, denominational activities, civic activities, and working with the various age groups at the church? Does the time allocation reflect your spiritual values?

What percentage of your day or week do you spend watching television, reading, or on the Internet (in nonwork-related activities)?

What percentage of your day or week do you spend on relationships: children, grandchildren, spouse or partner, friends, and other social activities? Are you emotionally present with your significant others, or do you time-share, consulting the Internet and texting while being with family members?

What would your perfect day or week look like as you dynamically balance ministry, self-care, family, relationships, and so forth?

Prayerfully look at the time of your life, inviting God to guide your decision making. Without reflection, there cannot be transformation. In the reflection, you can learn new ways to transform time and discover abundance in what previously looked cramped and scarce.

8

IGNITING YOUR SPIRIT

At that place he came to a cave, and spent the night there. Then the word of the LORD came to him, saying, "What are you doing here, Elijah?" He answered, "I have been very zealous for the LORD, the God of hosts; for the Israelites have forsaken your covenant, thrown down your altars, and killed your prophets with the sword. I alone am left, and they are seeking my life, to take it away." He said, "Go out and stand on the mountain before the LORD, for the LORD is about to pass by." Now there was a great wind, so strong that it was splitting mountains and breaking rocks in pieces before the LORD, but the LORD was not in the wind; and after the wind an earthquake, but the LORD was not in the earthquake; and after the earthquake a fire, but the LORD was not in the fire; and after the fire a sound of sheer silence.

—1 Kings 19:9–12

THE PASTOR AS MYSTIC, PROPHET, AND SHAMAN

Today's pastors are the spiritual children of the mystics, prophets, and shaman. Our spiritual heritage finds its energy in the lives of people who walked and talked with God. While we cannot claim to know the historicity of the biblical narratives in their entirety or even verify the historical existence of certain biblical figures, the biblical stories point to the reality of a spiritual dimension that is intimately related to our daily lives. By whatever images Scripture employs, it affirms that the

Holy One moves through all things, seeking good and not evil, guiding but not controlling the historical process, and searching for people who will awaken themselves and the world to divine word and wisdom.

Abraham and Sarah are visited by angelic beings and inspired by a voice and vision to leave their familiar homeland for land of promise and possibility. Jacob dreams of a ladder of angels and wrestles with a nocturnal stranger, receiving a mission, blessing, and wound. Joseph has life-transforming dreams, revealing insights about the unfolding of his global history. Isaiah encounters the Holy One in the Jerusalem temple and discovers that mysticism leads to mission. The Gospels and Acts of the Apostles invite us to see divine inspiration and energy everywhere: diseases are cured, spirits find healing, flames and winds enlighten, enliven, and inspire; dreams transform racists into universalists; and stars and dreams guide strangers from the East. The Pauline Epistles tell of the spiritual adventures of communities and affirm that God's good work is growing within our lives and communities. The epistle of James's counterpoint describes a holistic spirituality in which our beliefs and actions shape one another for the well-being of our communities and the world. Even the book of Revelation, often buried in pseudo-mathematical calculations, begins with a spiritual leader's vision and concludes with the promise that God will make all things new.

As many suggest, we are entering a time of "Great Emergence," "A Fifth Great Awakening," and an "Age of Transformation." Science is studying the sacred and discovering the significance of spirituality in promoting positive health outcomes. Studies indicate the possibility that intercessory prayer, or nonlocal causation, may be a factor in shaping people's lives despite geographical distance. Pluralism is adding to, rather than subtracting from, the Christian spiritual practices available to us. The Pew Forum for Religion and Public Life reports that 50 percent of North Americans claim to have had mystical experiences, that is, experiences of something transcendent and nonrational. Within and beyond the church, people claim to be on journeys, often with little or no guidance, but still ardent in looking for God by whatever pathways promise peace, ecstasy, meaning, and purpose.

Today's pastors wear the mantle of spirit persons from Abraham and Moses to Jesus and Paul, not to mention Mary of Nazareth and the woman with the flow of blood and countless unnamed women who encountered the Holy One and were forever changed. As spirit persons, pastors are called to enable people to experience God as a result of their own sense of divine intimacy and immediacy. As children of the shaman, they bear the responsibility of lifting up the prayers of the community and aligning humankind with its cosmic environment. Although today's pastors recognize that spiritual vitality is a community responsibility, it is, nevertheless, clear that without an experience of the holy— and there are many types of experiences of the Divine, based on personality type, temperament, life experience, and religious tradition—it is unlikely that pastors can nurture their congregants' spiritual growth.

Sadly, theological education is often more oriented toward the head than the heart and the rational than the mystical. Many students claim that they had a richer experience of God before they encountered the rationalist and deconstructionist biases of the academy. One of the most critical questions today's seminarians and pastors face is, how can I become a spirit person, whose encounter with the wellsprings of Life energizes me for healing and wholeness in ministry? Moreover, how can I balance head, heart, and hands as I embrace a practical mysticism that joins action with contemplation and rationalism with mystery? Perhaps more crucial at certain times of our ministerial lives, we must ask, how do we sustain a relationship with God amid frenetic voices of anxious congregants, dwindling resources, and greater responsibilities? How do we, within the storm, attend to the sheer silence of God from which the universe and each moment emerges? What spiritual practices illumine and energize both pastors and congregants? In many ways, this chapter expands on and deepens the previous chapter on time. Spiritual practices demand time commitment, and they also change our perception of time. Spiritual practices open us to new energies and awaken us to a larger perspective on life and our place in our community and the universe.

INTERACTIVE SPIRITUALITY

For decades I read Mark's account of the feeding of thousands without recognizing its importance as a model of healthy ministerial self-care. Listen to these words in the spirit of lectio divina, taking time to let God's voice speak within your spirit as you meditate upon these holy words.

The apostles gathered around Jesus, and told him all that they had done and taught. He said to them, "Come away to a deserted place all by yourselves and rest a while." For many were coming and going, and they had no leisure even to eat. And they went away in the boat to a deserted place by themselves. Now many saw them going and recognized them, and they hurried there on foot from all the towns and arrived ahead of them. As he went ashore, he saw a great crowd; and he had compassion for them, because they were like sheep without a shepherd; and he began to teach them many things. . . . Immediately he made his disciples get into the boat and go on ahead to the other side, to Bethsaida, while he dismissed the crowd. After saying farewell to them, he went up on the mountain to pray.

—Mark 6:30–34, 45–46

What did you notice about this passage? Did you notice anything that might change your understanding of ministry and the relationship of action and contemplation? Do the images of Scripture mirror your own experiences as a working pastor, whether solo, on a multiple staff, or bivocational?

A few years back, when I was preparing to teach a session focusing on Mark 6, the following passage leaped out at me: "He said to them, 'Come away to a deserted place all by yourselves and rest a while.' For many were coming and going, and they had no leisure even to eat." (v. 31). The disciples had just returned from their first successful teaching and healing mission; not on their own but going two by two. They returned not only elated but also fatigued from weeks devoted to healing and teaching. Nothing succeeds like success in ministry. The more gifted you are, the greater demand on your time and energy. Effective pastors are immersed in relationships and constantly interacting with the culture and community around them. But, to stay fresh and vital in ministry, and to remain connected to the wellsprings of divine energy, we need to say no to some things to say yes to others. Despite the fact that the needs were great, Jesus does something counterintuitive: he takes his disciples on retreat. Jesus recognizes that spiritual centeredness is essential to healthy ministry and that regardless of their commitment and good intentions, his disciples are running on empty.

The Gospels include few if any throw-away lines. I am sure that Mark was addressing the fatigue that even the most loyal and effective disciples feel. There is so much urgent demand and often not enough hours in the day. We want to do more, but we need to return to stillness to find the energy to claim our mantle as healers and spirit persons.

What is also striking about this passage is that it begins and ends in prayer. Once the people are fed, Jesus sends everyone away, including his closest followers, and then takes time to go up a mountain to pray. The healer and spirit person, to use the language of theologian and New Testament scholar Marcus Borg, needed to connect to the vine of divine energy and inspiration to maintain his own effectiveness in ministry. Embracing relatedness to others required enhancing his relatedness to God.

We don't know how long this retreat lasted nor do we know the content of their time apart. My suspicion is that it was a bit like the best of my retreats with students in my role as a university chaplain or retreats I often spend with pastors. We ate a good meal, shared stories and laughs, and then spent time in prayer and spiritual conversation. The interplay of companionship and silence, of extroversion and introversion, restored my students' and pastoral colleagues' spirits and physical well-being, and that same interplay renewed Jesus's first followers.

Jesus himself may have needed spiritual and physical renewal. Mark notes that while his disciples were on their preaching tour, Jesus's cousin and, I believe, close spiritual friend John the Baptist had just been murdered. Jesus may have been worn down by his own grief. He may have felt the emptiness of losing a spiritual friend to meaningless, violent death. But that retreat changed everything. When he sees the crowd, Jesus's heart is opened to them: as the Scripture says, "As he went ashore, he saw a great crowd; and he had compassion for them, because they were like sheep without a shepherd; and he began to teach them many things" (v. 34). The key word is compassion, the heartfelt intimacy that comes from renewal and reconnection with the divine "vine," to the Energy of Love. His whole being refreshed, Jesus was able to address the needs of others with compassion. He also may have gained new perspective from his time apart: rather than panicking when the disciples reported that they lacked the provisions to feed the multitude, Jesus imagined the possibility that within the few loaves of bread and fish were the resources to feed a multitude.

For Jesus, like ourselves, spiritual centeredness awakens us to what social scientist and futurist Willis Harmon describes as "the higher creativity" and the envisagement of novel possibilities and the energy to embody them. The needs will always be great and we will be tempted to place our spiritual lives on the back burner; but deep down we know our vocation is to be people of spirit, who are most faithful and effective even in the politics of our communities when we are connected with God's creative and surprising love.

PATHWAYS OF THE SPIRIT

Some people might not consider spirituality as an essential element in self-care. They believe that our relationship to God and to others should be purely self-effacing. They assert that if we meditate or pray for our well-being, even if we are also actively praying and working for the well-being of others, our meditation and prayer becomes a matter of self-interest rather than sacrificial love. In contrast, I believe that Jesus's affirmation that we should love others with the same care as we love ourselves assumes a healthy relationship between spiritual practices, self-care, concern for others, and giving glory to God.

Holistic spiritual formation is about widening self-interest so that there is no ultimate dualism between our well-being and the well-being of others. Growing in wisdom and stature means that we see others' needs as being as important as our own. But to support their needs and insure a healthier world for our children and our children's children, we need to insure that God's abundant life continues to flow through us, and then toward others. We need to love our bodies enough to insure that we are healthy, strong, and energetic appropriate to our age and physical condition; and we need to love the bodies of others by seeking justice in our eating habits, economics, and political involvement. God delights, as Song of Solomon suggests, in sensuality, physical touch, and romance that bring joy and beauty to us and to God's experience of the world. As Mark 6 suggests, our own decision to withdraw temporarily from active social and religious involvement is essential to ongoing compassionate and imaginative activity on behalf of vulnerable people.

People who pray or meditate regularly are not "so heavenly minded that they are no earthly good," as the saying goes. Perhaps, those who are always on the go without replenishing themselves spiritually will end up as "no earthly good" as a result of compassion fatigue, ill health, and burnout. In fact, if God is providing us with visions of possibility for us and others and the energy to embody them in each given moment, then our spiritual attentiveness enables us to be more aligned with God's wisdom for issues of congregational life, justice seeking, and earth care.

There are many pathways of the Spirit appropriate to our age, education, personality type, professional setting, physical condition, and environment. Some of us experience God with our eyes wide open serving breakfast at the soup kitchen. Others encounter God, like Jacob and Joseph, by paying heed to the wisdom of the unconscious emerging from dreams. Still others, like me, find a sense of God's presence when we pause awhile every morning before beginning the adventures of a brand new day.

This text is grounded in the affirmation that spiritual practices awaken us to God's presence and vision of wholeness in the messy and complicated world of family life, conflict resolution, budget meetings, hospital visits, baptisms, friendships, self-affirmation, and funerals. Spirituality is not one more thing to do in an already-busy life; it is how we live our lives. It is our attentiveness to the voices of God encountering us through the voices of others, both human and nonhuman, and the affairs of institutions and nations. Spirituality involves being fully alive to our experience, the calling of the moment, the voices of children and elders, and the "sighs too deep for words" inspiring us to be faithful to God by our fidelity to the world (Rom. 8:26).

PRAY AS YOU CAN, NOT AS YOU CAN'T

In my many years of supporting pastoral excellence, self-care, and spiritual formation, I have heard many variations on the following lament: "I just can't sit down to pray. My mind wanders, the needs of the church and the world intrude, the tasks of the day call, and I want to get up and go after five minutes." I have also heard pastors complain, "My friends can't understand why I need to meditate and go away on contemplative retreats; they tell me that my spiritual practices are naval gazing and won't change the world." In response to both of these concerns, I remind my companions of the spiritual counsel "Pray as you can, not as you can't!" God loves diversity: we can see it in the hues of sunrise and sunset, the wondrous colors of flora and fauna, the cultures and ethnicity of humankind, expressions of art, sexuality, and spirituality, and in the varieties of personality types. The point of prayer and spiritual formation is to discover our own unique relationship with God and creation, not follow the exact pathways of others. Many of us need spiritual companions, whether a spiritual director or spiritual growth group, to help us discern the spiritual practices that fit our personality and life situation. To use the words of Frederick Buechner and Parker Palmer once again, finding the path to a holistic spirituality that brings beauty and justice to the world and well-being to us involves "listening to your life" and "letting your life speak."

While my own spiritual practice of quiet contemplation and walking prayer typifies an introvert's approach to experiencing God, I deeply appreciate more extroverted approaches, like my wife's and Roy's, a United Church of Christ pastor in Central Pennsylvania. Some of us find God in stillness, others in conversation. When I asked this high-functioning, on-the-go pastor about his spiritual practices, Roy responded without hesitation: "My spirit is enlightened each week when I meet with our Bible Buds every Tuesday morning." An ecumenist by nature and practice, Roy is delighted that the group is made up of Lutheran, Episcopalian, and United Church of Christ pastors. Each week this group meets to reflect on the lectionary as well as share the joys and challenges of ministry and family life. "I love it," Roy continues, "because there are many current and retired pastors. I have been blessed by having good relationships with mentors and colleagues in this group."

Spirituality is not just about the ethereal, disembodied soul; it is profoundly embodied in acts of justice as well as our own personal physical stewardship. Becky shares how important the practice of Reiki healing touch is in her spiritual life.[1] "Each day I spend fifteen minutes being still on my couch. I place my hands on various parts of my body, identified as energy centers and experience a deep calm and connection with all creation. I feel like the woman who was healed by touching Jesus; a quiet energy flows in me. I can't describe it, but it gives me calm and insight to face the day."

Reiki healing touch is essential to my own spiritual life. On the one hand, I experience the joy, calm, and energy of giving myself a Reiki treatment every afternoon. I have to confess that quite often I fall asleep. I don't bemoan this and assume there are good reasons for my soporific response—I need the rest and I know that the energy is still flowing even when I doze off for a few minutes. On the other hand, I regularly give Reiki treatments to friends and family members. I also give distant Reiki treatments to people in need. Similar to intercessory prayer, distant Reiki awakens the energy of love and healing in those who receive my treatments.

Jane, a bivocational Lutheran pastor, is a nature mystic. She laces up her boots and hits the trail with her Labrador retriever. According to Jane, "Contemplative time in nature is essential to balancing ministry and my law practice. I take my phone with me for safety reasons, but turn it off. My house is just two miles from the woods, so I'm able to take an hour hike every other day. During the summer, I go with a group of friends on weeklong hiking trips. I have a busy mind, but after a few minutes in the woods, my mind slows down and I just dwell in the moment."

Sylvia, an Episcopal priest and mother of three children, ages three to eight, admits that balancing ministry, parenting, and prayer is challenging. At first she gave up on spiritual practices, believing that a dedicated prayer life would be impossible until all her children were in school. Then, as Sylvia relates, "everything changed when I heard a lecturer on spiritual growth state that some prayer is better than none. I realized that I could take five minutes before the kids wake up in the morning. I could also take a few breaths and listen to calm music and hymns in the car after I drop off the kids at school and day care. I've learned that I can pray on the run at stoplights, and when I watch my children run from the car to school, I can bless them."

The following story, told in variety of ways, is a challenge to the constantly on-the-go pastor. A wealthy American businessman was on safari and, given his purpose-driven personality, he wanted to cover as much ground as possible each day. After several days of marching, he was surprised and then angry when one morning the porters refused to move. Finally he asked the head porter what was going on, "We're wasting valuable time. Why are the men just sitting around the trees?" The head porter, who alone spoke English, responded, "We've been moving so fast that we need to rest for a day to let our souls catch up with our bodies." That's the pace of life for many pastors, isn't it? To be spirit-centered ministers, we need to let our souls catch up with our bodies, and this means pausing awhile to open to God's guidance and energy.

Stacy takes that story to heart. She is a lively, extroverted mother of three, who also happens to be the senior pastor of a midsized California congregation. Deeply involved in social justice issues, especially the hard issues of immigration and human trafficking, Stacy was on the verge of "brown out," as she recalls. "I loved my work, putting the gospel in practice. I could balance fifteen things and still be energized. But my body and soul finally came to a halt. I recognized that even an extrovert like me can't burn the ministerial candle at both ends. It's tough, but I'm learning a new kind of spirituality, one that contemplates and then acts. I stop to smell the roses—and they are my three children and husband. Sometimes I just sit in my wing chair and watch them, grateful for all the love in this family. When I get to the church, I don't sweep through like a hurricane anymore. I come a little later now, after spending some time with the Bible each morning. This quiet study and prayer time has transformed my spirit and sermons." No longer a tsunami storming into her office with lots of ideas, many of which wear out her colleagues, she lets others speak first and listens before she plunges into the latest new ideas. "My colleagues no longer run when they see me coming. I think a lot of this is a result of slowing down, reflecting on Scripture, and beginning the day with a sense of calm rather than haste." She also admits that her husband's support has been essential to her spiritual practices. "My husband has really stepped up: most days he gets the children ready for school and on Saturday mornings he takes them to the park; Sunday mornings, he makes breakfast, gets them dressed." A number of men have also expressed gratitude for their spouse's willingness to give them time for prayer and meditation.

Variations in one's focus in ministry can also be a source of spiritual formation. When the land lies fallow, it becomes more fertile for the next planting. This is the case for Lucy, another bivocational pastor, who notes, "Ironically, my other job in institutional technology keeps me balanced as well. I thought it was a good idea, because it makes it possible to serve a tiny but wonderful church that can't afford a full-time pastor, but it also makes my mind work in different ways, and it includes occasional travel to big cities from my rural congregations. It helps keep me real and fresh." Lucy sees God in the people she works with in business and in the faces of the children at church.

Pastors responding to my questions made it clear that often extroverts feel disenfranchised by "old school, one-size-fits-all" approaches to spiritual formation. Ted says, "There's no way I could sit for centering prayer for fifteen minutes. That would kill me. I listen to music and it restores my soul. I bounce around to jazz and hip-hop or float away with classical. I feel God's passion in the musical rhythm and God's healing energy in the tune."

Steve avers, "In seminary I was regularly disappointed that the spiritual retreats failed to reach me in a meaningful way. These were centered on silence, art, and finding a place apart. Then I stumbled across an article on the differences in spiritual practices among introverts and extroverts. I no longer felt like I was a failure at spirituality. I'm an extrovert and I get most of my spiritual experiences in community. I have to be intentional, however. I find that praying for and with folks and teaching adult classes ignite my spirit, along with occasional deep movements of the Spirit during preaching."[2]

HEALTHY PRACTICES FOR HEALTHY MINISTERS

Spiritual practices embrace the gifts of both introverts and extroverts. Introverts, like myself, tend toward quiet forms of meditation. Introverts enjoy listening to God's still, small voice, speaking through "sighs too deep for words" (Rom. 8:26). Extroverts, like my wife, Kate, tend toward active forms of meditation such as chanting or sung prayers, body prayers, and prayer with open eyes.

Kate Epperly is a kitchen mystic and garden meditator. She feels closest to God amid the pots and pans or working in the garden. She has never found it easy to practice various forms of "sitting, eyes-closed" contemplative prayers. She likes to sing her prayers or pray as she enjoys the flora and fauna of the natural world. Literary in spirit, Kate has found journaling an important way of opening to God's Spirit. Often when I return home from my morning meditative walks, I find Kate on the balcony quietly writing in her journal as she bathes her eyes on the beauties of the morning.

In contrast, many more-introverted people like myself prefer contemplative prayer and quiet walks. I realize that my approach is unique: not everyone has the leisure for long walks and meditation each day, given the responsibilities of family life. However, I have found that most congregational pastors can take at least half an hour for spiritual growth each day. It's a matter of choice and commitment.

Centering Prayer

I first encountered a version of centering prayer when I learned Transcendental Meditation in 1970 at a meditation ashram in Berkeley, California. I learned Christian centering prayer a few years later. Both types of meditation have been central to deepening my spiritual growth and awakening me to God's presence in the many and varied events of life.

In the practice of centering prayer, the contemplative pastor begins by finding a comfortable position—a yoga position or a comfortable chair, with feet placed on the floor.

After a few moments of stillness, pause to breathe deeply the presence of God's breath breathing through your life. Turn your attention to your prayer phrase or word, a simple, rhythmic word or sentence. In the spirit of the spiritual classic *The Cloud of Unknowing*, thought to be influential in the origins of centering prayer, your prayer word is a searchlight that illuminates yourself and God's self moving within you.

When your mind wanders, simply return to your prayer word without any sense of judgment. Experience a sense of God's presence, flowing in and through your body, mind, and spirit. While a short time spent in meditation is always better than none, most centering prayer teachers suggest that you pause for centering prayer twice daily for a period of fifteen or twenty minutes.

Praying with Your Eyes Open

Extroverted people tend toward imagistic and relational forms of meditation. Meditative practices can stimulate as well as calm and enable us to experience the holiness of chaos as well as regularity. In this type of prayer, similar to centering prayer in its focus but external in direction, the practitioner experiences God in people, places, and things. It involves looking deeply into your encounters for the Divine within. Prayer with your eyes open joins the inner and outer journeys, awakening us to God in all things and all things in God.

In this exercise, look deeply into everything you encounter throughout the day. Look for God in all God's disguises, whether attractive or distressing. Similar to experiences of centering prayer, most people experience distractions. Forgetting our spiritual intentions happens to most of us at times; we become inattentive to beauty, wonder, and joy. We forget the Divine within us and others. Again, without judgment, return to a prayerful attitude toward everyone you meet.

The Way of Blessing

A variation on this practice is the way of blessing. In the blessing prayer, you make a commitment to bless everyone you meet. Let your hello be a prayer and your thank you be an intercession. Let your "Have a beautiful day!" be a blessing. Whether you tend toward introversion or extroversion, the point of spiritual practices is to experience holiness in all things and to weave your day into a fabric of worship, holiness, and service.

9

SETTING YOUR SPIRITUAL GPS

That evening, at sundown, they brought to him all who were sick or possessed with demons. And the whole city was gathered around the door. And he cured many who were sick with various diseases, and cast out many demons; and he would not permit the demons to speak, because they knew him. In the morning, while it was still very dark, he got up and went out to a deserted place, and there he prayed. And Simon and his companions hunted for him. When they found him, they said to him, "Everyone is searching for you." He answered, "Let us go on to the neighboring towns, so that I may proclaim the message there also; for that is what I came out to do." And he went throughout Galilee, proclaiming the message in their synagogues and casting out demons.

—Mark 1:32–39

GUIDED BY A VISION

Having a vision

I must confess that I seldom use the King James Version for research or writing. But every so often, its translations trump the alternatives. As I stated early in this book, I believe that King James has it right for Proverbs 29:18, spiritually and practically speaking, even if it may not be the most accurate translation. "Where there is no vision, the people perish." The Common English Bible adds a nuance, "When there's no vision, the people get out of control."

Healthy ministry is guided by personal and professional visions or guiding principles. A fluid and evolving vision serves as the horizon that guides our ministry and enables us to prioritize our personal and professional lives. In the biblical tradition, visions emerge in the synergy of divine-human partnership. The biblical tradition describes the ongoing human response to an active and intimately involved God who presents individuals and nations with an array of possibilities for the long haul as well as each moment, appropriate to their particular historical context. The preceding passage from Mark 1 highlights the role of Jesus's vocational vision in shaping the course of his ministry. According to Mark, Jesus is just beginning his ministry: Mark in quick order describes Jesus's baptism by John the Baptist, Jesus's wilderness retreat to discern the nature of his calling, Jesus's proclamation of God's realm, and a day in the life of Jesus. After teaching, preaching, and healing all day, Jesus arises early and goes to a quiet place to pray. But, typical of the experience of many pastors, Jesus's prayer time is interrupted by his anxious disciples, urgently reminding him that he has more work to do in Capernaum. The needs of the village are great and, as a complementary passage from Luke 4:42–44 suggests, the people want him to stay to be their resident rabbi and healer. Despite the adulation and appreciation, Jesus makes what appears to be a blunt and thoughtless response:[38] "Let us go on to the neighboring towns, so that I may proclaim the message there also; for that is what I came out to do" (v. 38). Mark's version concludes with the following description of Jesus's vocational vision, "[39]And he went throughout Galilee, proclaiming the message in their synagogues and casting out demons."

The key phrase for pastors today is "for that is what I came out to do." While Jesus doesn't explicitly state his vision, it is clear that his decisions are guided by his vocational vision as a messenger of God's realm. Jesus is willing to disappoint the members of the community and leave some tasks undone in order to be faithful to the vision he has received in dialogue with his Loving Parent.

Jesus's prayerful response to his eager followers begs the questions, What is your vision of ministry? What practices enable you to discern God's calling for your life and ministry? Are you listening to God's voice as well as your own and the voices of your congregation in charting your vision?

what is our priority or priorities

DISCOVERING WHAT'S IMPORTANT IN LIFE AND MINISTRY

The Gospels record two clear vision statements from Jesus. In John 10:10 Jesus affirms "I came that they might have life, and have it abundantly." While Jesus's vision statement is vague in its detail, it clearly states that Jesus and his Divine Parent support abundance, health, and well-being in all that they do. You can imagine Jesus making decisions based on the following question: "Does this course of action promote abundant life in the short term and long term?" Luke narrates Jesus's use of Isaiah 61:1–2 as the centerpiece of his gospel vision:

> The Spirit of the Lord is upon me, because he has anointed me to bring good news to the poor. He has sent me to proclaim release to the captives and recovery of sight to the blind, to let the oppressed go free, to proclaim the year of the Lord's favor.
>
> —Luke 4:18–19

Luke's description of Jesus's vision statement joins tradition and innovation. Jesus grounds his mission directly in the prophetic tradition. His message and ministry will holistically join personal and social healing and transformation. Jesus is innovative in his use of Isaiah. While he clearly roots himself in the prophet tradition's vision of justice, he stops his proclamation at "the year of the Lord's favor," the jubilee year in which the social order is restructured to reflect God's shalom for the poor as well as the rich. All will have the possibility of abundant life. But Jesus does not include Isaiah's next words: "and the day of vengeance of our God" (Isa. 61:2). Jesus's sense of mission and focus on healing exclude vengeance as a primary attribute of God's relationship to humankind. Jesus recognized that our actions have consequences, but even when we turn away from God, God is still seeking our wholeness and abundant life, as revealed in Jesus's parables of a shepherd looking for a lost sheep, a woman looking for a coin, or a father and mother celebrating their child's return. Jesus's radical hospitality included the tax collector Zacchaeus, the rich young ruler, and a military leader of the occupying troops as well as prostitutes, sight-impaired people, and women with diseases that rendered them socially and religiously unclean.

In light of Jesus's vision statements, consider for a moment the vision that guides your personal and professional life. Do you have a vision statement? Have you considered your life mission as evidenced in the mission of each moment? Our personal visions are a matter of call and response, and discovery and creativity. In the spirit of the Scriptures, I believe that God is constantly inviting us to be companions in healing the world. The shape of God's quest and our response is related to our age, life situation, and personal and professional context. In prayerful openness, we discover God's vision—or better yet, visions—for our life. But in the discovery we are called to be God's partners in shaping this vision over the long haul and one moment at a time. Healthy ministry is creative rather than passive in its response to God's inspiration. When we awaken to God's visions for our life and this moment in time, we expand our creativity and agency.

The adventurous nature of visionary ministry can be described by the following imaginative questions from God to each of us. After presenting us with visions for our life to be lived out in macrocosm as well as microcosm, God addresses us: "Here are some dreams I have for your life, what are you going to do about them? How will you make them your own? How will you claim your role as my partner in the quest for shalom at this point of your life?"

Jesus's vision of his calling as God's beloved child, teacher, and healer enabled him to discover his priorities in ministry. He could have sought the comfort of being chaplain to the people of Capernaum, but he recognized that God's call had a global dimension, and that reality pushed him beyond the comfort zone of his own ethnic group and the religious mores of his community.

In reflecting on his pastoral vision to "bring healing and wholeness to his congregation and the world," Sidney, a recently ordained United Methodist pastor, affirms that "having a vision, even a simple one, serves as my daily moral and professional compass. Sure, I have to pay the rent at the church and do all sorts of things that don't appear to have anything to do with my mission statement, but having a vision of healing and wholeness guides my behavior, keeps me from getting lost in the minutiae, and helps me realize that even small things like the condition of bathrooms or arriving on time to meetings are part of my commitment to being a healing partner." A Lutheran pastor, also in her first congregational call, Deborah agrees, "My mission, based on Jesus's sermon in Luke 4, guides how my approach to leadership and business as well as pastoral care and preaching. I have found that so many of my colleagues forget issues of justice and healing when it comes to staff management and budget issues. I'm tempted to follow my agenda at the expense of my colleagues' feelings, but then I remember Jesus's words about liberation, good news, and healing and realize that justice begins at home and in the office. My pastoral vision relates to everything I do, not just the obvious aspects of ministry."

A Disciples of Christ pastor, Tim notes, "I used to drift through my ministry, going from day to day, but when I wrote up my own mission statement, I began to be more focused and effective in ministry. I follow through on commitments better and get my work done on time. Sure, I'm a Myers-Briggs 'perceiving type,' so I go with the flow, but now I have a sense of where the flow is going! I wouldn't make it with a fancy statement: it's simply 'I share God's vision of shalom in every aspect of my life—in teaching and preaching, administration, spiritual leadership, and family life.' I work out the details in real time."

CHARTING A VISION

The Old Testament prophet Habakkuk receives a word from God: "Write the vision; make it plain on tablets, so that a runner may read it" (Hab. 2:2). Visions, like spiritual affirmations, don't have to be long or complicated. While Mark doesn't report the nature of the vision that motivated Jesus to leave Capernaum to share God's good news with other towns, we can suspect that it might have been a variation of the message he proclaimed as he began his ministry: "The time is fulfilled, and the kingdom of God has come near; repent, and believe in the good news" (Mark 1:15). Perhaps, it was something as simple as the Gospel of John's report of Jesus's vision statement "I have come that they might have life, and have it abundantly." It might have been "I share God's good news that transforms people's lives, mind, body, spirit, and relationships."

Returning to the question I asked earlier in this chapter, take a moment to respond to the following questions with pen in hand: What is your vision? Can you write it down in a sentence or two?

Habakkuk notes three important things about any vision statement. First, articulate the vision that you are receiving in the dynamic process of God's call and your response. Speak it out loud. Hear its words transform your life, giving you direction as you journey toward the far horizons of your personal and professional life. Second, write it down. My experience is that people truly begin to take seriously their visions when they commit them to writing. The vision remains ungrounded until you carefully examine the words and the images it evokes. Finally, make it simple so that (1) you can remember and repeat it throughout the day and (2) you can share it with others, if the occasion arises. Flexibility is essential, because your vision is always embodied in concrete situations and in relationship with unique and concrete people and situations. In fact, most of us learn the nature of our visions as we go along in life, testing them by our responses to particular situations. Building on Habakkuk's guidance, the third aspect of charting a vision is to pray your visions. Ask God to help you live your vision in the concrete world and be willing to expand your vision as new situations arise. Finally, create an affirmation from your vision statement. For example, Jesus's statement in John 10:10 can be affirmed in the following words, spoken throughout the day: "I bring God's abundant life to every situation and encounter" or "I am a messenger of divine abundance wherever I go." Living by Habakkuk's approach will transform your life and ministry.

A key element in my personal and professional vision is "to be an agent of God's blessing." This means different things in different settings. As I interact with my grandchildren, it means that I give them my full attention as I read with them, play games with them, or put them to bed. As I write this text, it means that my goal is to create something accessible and relevant so that it will bless your life and ministry and awaken you to new images of health, wholeness, and excellence in personal, professional, and relational life. The vision of blessing shapes how I behave as well as what I say. I regularly ask myself the following question: Do my words and actions bring healing and beauty to the world? Do my encounters help people experience greater joy and meaning? Do I add something beautiful to God's experience of the world? I also regularly say the following affirmation: "I bless everyone I meet" to keep me on course throughout the day, especially when I feel myself succumbing to alienation and polarization.

My commitment to bless is part of a larger vision that I seek to embody: "I bring beauty, healing, transformation, and blessing to the world and to everyone I meet as a pastor, teacher, writer, and companion. I bring beauty, healing, and transformation to students, program participants, grandchildren, children, my wife, congregants, readers, and so forth." Concretely, this means that as I write these words an hour before sunrise in my study in Chevy Chase, Maryland, I am implicitly imagining you reading this text. I don't know your name, but my vision is to bring beauty, healing, transformation, and blessing into your life by writing these words you are reading right now. It is my prayer that you receive this blessing and that my counsel positively shapes your own unique process of being faithful to God's calling.

Living by a vision also shapes the microworld of personal encounters lived out moment by moment. Our personal vision is lived out throughout the day and in the lively call and response of God and the world. Each moment has its own vocation as part of God's quest to heal the world through partnership with humankind and most particularly this human—you or me—right here and how.

Many of us wonder how to chart a vision. Once again, there are many ways to discover your vision for this time of your life. They will depend on your personality type, relationships, experience, and context. Here are a few ways to chart a vision for your life and ministry.

A Vision Retreat

I believe that the accounts of Jesus's wilderness temptations are often misnamed; I believe Jesus went to the wilderness for a spiritual vision quest. Jesus's sojourn in the wilderness did involve facing temptation, but more important, it involved claiming his vision as God's messenger of good news to humankind and, I believe, the nonhuman world. In Mark's shorthand fashion (Mark 1:9–15), Jesus hears God's word of affirmation immediately following his baptism. This word confirms his nonnegotiable relationship with his Divine Parent: "You are my beloved child; I am pleased with your life." In addition to this affirmation, he receives the energy and guidance of the Spirit that "drove" or "lured" him into the wilderness for a spiritual retreat to ground, deepen, and claim his visionary experience as the foundation of his lifework. He was not alone on his retreat. Mark notes that "angels waited on him"; that is, our times of discerning God's vision are never solitary but accompanied by divine word and wisdom embodied in the messengers God provides for us in people and in synchronous encounters. Finally, Jesus returns to the challenges of embodying his vision, his timing is possibly motivated by his spiritual companion John the Baptist's arrest. Visionary experiences and affirmations always occur in time and space; they are always contextual and related to our personal and professional circumstances. Upon his return to the community, Jesus announces his purpose for beginning his ministry: "The time is fulfilled, and the kingdom of God has come near; repent, and believe the good news" (v. 15). Jesus's good news is embodied in a day of preaching and healing and his willingness to differentiate himself from others—proclaiming the message is "what I came out to do" (Mark 1:38)—by going to neighboring towns rather than establishing a successful ministry in Capernaum.

More introverted pastors may choose a physical time away periodically to discern, explore, articulate, and ponder embodying their vision. Such retreats can occur at monasteries and retreat centers, long hikes in the woods, or a series of hourly visits over a week or two to a quiet place, depending on one's life situation. Jeremy notes that spending a week at a Jesuit retreat center in Central Pennsylvania transformed his life and ministry: "I was floundering and uncertain of my calling, but in that week, the pieces began to fit together. I saw that God was leading me to a truly healthy and mission-oriented ministry. I didn't have a mystical experience, but I felt a stirring that I could articulate. My mission is to bring love and justice to my family and to my church. I am called to embody the love I preach at home and to preach that love at church to inspire people to reach out to our neighborhood."

Spiritual Direction

Yesterday morning, I sat with a pastor who had run out of fuel in his last congregation and was wondering what to do now that his sabbatical was concluding. He didn't want to repeat the process of overwork and burnout again. He confessed that the sabbatical came "in the nick of time." We prayed and joined in breath prayer, and in the call and response of spiritual direction, I asked questions and prayerfully listened to the "sighs too deep for words" emerging in his responses (Rom. 8:26). We prayed for healing and transformation and new life in ministry.

One-to-one spiritual direction can be a powerful inspiration in discerning your vision for personal and professional life. With a prayerful companion whose task is to listen with you in God's presence, you discover insights and possibilities that would unlikely occur in the everyday maelstrom of pastoral and family life. Spiritual direction creates a healing space-time for creative transformation. In the stillness you may experience God's voice speaking in and through the deepest desires of your heart. You may discover, in trusting the confidentiality of a trusted spiritual friend, that you can be yourself, share your challenges without judgment, and experience enough light to guide you to the next steps of your ministry.

Sheryl recalls going to her spiritual director completely "at a loss about the future of her ministry. I felt harried and bogged down. Although I appeared to be effective, I realized that I was in maintenance mode. I was giving adequate sermons and leadership, but I didn't feel any inspiration in my work or congregation. I needed new life and a way ahead." After several monthly sessions, Sheryl gradually discovered a vision emerging that involved a lively blend of dynamic worship, outreach to the community, and a commitment to spiritual growth in the congregation. "I falter from time to time," Sheryl admits, "but just that simple vision of journey inward and outward in prayer and study gave me a polestar for leading my congregation and they are helping me shape this vision by their input and commitment." Sheryl's work with her spiritual director taught her something important about visioning: visions are never static but always emerging and evolving.

While we may appreciate Stephen Covey's "begin with the end in mind" as a catalyst for transformation, the horizon is always moving, a healthy vision never stays put but guides us forward toward new adventures. In the spirit of the saying *solvitur ambulando* ("It is solved in the walking"), a vision is always on the way, in process, and in its incompleteness gives birth to multiple and evolving visions appropriate for new occasions and challenges.

A Clearness Committee

The Society of Friends, or Quakers, have long championed a form of group spiritual direction, the clearness committee, as a pathway for personal and vocational discernment. Profoundly theological in nature, the clearness committee presumes that God is speaking to each one of us individually and in community, giving us the guidance we need to fulfill God's vision for us. God's inner light, as the Quakers say, radiates from within each one of us, giving us illumination for one step at a time and often helping us make a way when there appears to be no way forward. This light, however, is often hidden by the many voices of our past, ego needs, fears, and the society around us. We often need a village to raise up our inner light so that it illumines our vocational path. In the words of Parker Palmer:

> Behind the Clearness Committee is a simple but crucial conviction: each of us has an inner teacher, a voice of truth, that offers the guidance and power we need to deal with our problems. But that inner voice is often garbled by various kinds of inward and outward interference. The function of the Clearness Committee is not to give advice or "fix" people from the outside in but rather to help people remove the interference so that they can discover their own wisdom from the inside out. If we do not believe in the reality of inner wisdom, the Clearness Committee can become an opportunity for manipulation. But if we respect the power of the inner teacher, the Clearness Committee can be a remarkable way to help someone name and claim his or her deepest truth. [1]

The key element of a clearness committee is that you gather a community of trusted and spiritually grounded friends. Prayerful in approach and trusting the inner wisdom of the people involved, members of the clearness committee covenant to simply ask open-ended and spiritually grounded questions aimed at eliciting the deepest wisdom of the person seeking guidance. Trusting the wisdom of the person seeking guidance, the members do not advise, coach, or teach in the course of the meeting; they listen for God's call in the questions and responses.

Steve found the caring questions of the clearness committee a source of insight as he pondered whether to stay in his current congregation or to place his name in his denomination's search and call process. "What I was really looking for was a vision that would give me insight into whether to go or stay. I discovered in the process that God still had plans for me in this church. I was called to bring them consistent, caring, and courageous leadership. I saw my vocation there as reminding them that God loved them, gave them gifts for ministry, and that these gifts were intended for mission. In the process of finding a renewed vision, I discovered something important about myself. I had let my vision get bogged down because I didn't take enough time away from church for prayer and personal refreshment, especially with my wife and children. If I was to grow in my call, I needed to keep clear boundaries of work and family and find time for daily prayer and exercise. I found out through their compassionate questions that not doing explicit ministry was as important as doing ministry for following my call."

Appreciative Visioning for Pastors

Focus on what doing — the positive not the negative

The practice of appreciative inquiry has been transformational for many congregations as they seek to articulate and live by a vision. While many approaches to change begin with the questions, What's wrong? or What's the problem?, appreciative inquiry begins with an affirmative approach, both personally and organizationally. The key questions are, Where's your passion? What's your joy and passion in life and in work? What are your successes? In *Tending to the Holy*, Kate Epperly and I share a visioning approach based on the insights of appreciative inquiry, involving the following:

- Remembering life-giving moments in which you experienced God's presence in your life
- Remembering life-giving moments in ministry in which you felt fully alive in your ministerial tasks
- Acknowledging what you value most in your life and ministry, based on these life-giving and passion-filled moments
- Reflecting on how you might build on these life-giving moments and passions
- Writing down a vision statement grounded in the first four steps
- Drawing a picture or visualizing the vision
- Reflecting on first steps in actualizing your vision[2]

Appreciative visioning is grounded in a clear affirmation of God's abundant life and inspiration flowing in and through us. It reminds us that regardless of the circumstances of our life and ministry, we have the power to choose our responses and that this power is energized by evolving and enlivening spiritual visions. Recognizing the graceful interdependence of life, visionary pastors live out Dag Hammarskjold's affirmation:

> For all that has been—Thanks!
> For all that shall be—Yes![3]

VISION, PRIORITIES, AND CONFLICT

All things flow, as the ancient Greek philosopher Heraclitus observed. Whether in ministry or daily life, we can't step into the same waters twice. The dynamic movements of life call pastors to be creative, inventive, and flexible in charting and embodying their visions. I often tell people with whom I work that "I have a vision and not an agenda." If there is any problem inherent in Stephen Covey's perceptive counsel to "begin with the end in mind," it is found in the reality that our goals need to be flexibly, rather than absolutely, embodied in an ever-changing world. Still, without a flexible and evolving vision, we are at the mercy of external events and our own moods and inclinations. A vision orients us toward the far shore, even when we—like the magi who visited the toddler Jesus—have to return home by a different route than we previously imagined.

A flexible vision is essential to give shape to our vocation on a daily basis, to remind us what is truly important in life, and to enable us to more creatively deal with conflict situations, when we must ask ourselves, Are our behaviors in times of congregational conflict congruent with our personal and professional vision? In the spirit of congregational and family systems theory, charting a flexible vision enables us to be "in but not of" our congregation's life, it helps us maintain the fine balance between relational intimacy and professional integrity that we see in Jesus's response to his disciples.

Nothing was inherently wrong with the disciples' request that Jesus return to the village as teacher, healer, and chaplain, but it was not congruent with Jesus's global vision. Jesus differentiated himself from his anxious disciples while maintaining the intimacy of his relationship as their spiritual teacher. Jesus invited them to experience his vision as a pathway forward that would creatively transform their lives as well as the lives of vulnerable, oppressed, and ostracized people throughout Galilee.

In one of Plato's dialogues, the great teacher Socrates asks young Phaedo, "Where have you been and where are you going?" A flexible vision orients and prioritizes our commitments and foci—it helps us connect where we've been with where we hope to be going. A United Church of Christ pastor, Stephen asserts that having a vision for his life and ministry has been pivotal in insuring his personal and professional well-being. "My vision is to be a loving father, husband, friend, and pastor whose commitment to God is revealed in every aspect of my life. I seek to be an agent in God's vision of shalom." For Stephen, shalom means "wholeness, justice, and peace" and this means that he seeks to be "faithful to my family, my church, the community, and myself."

Prone to burnout that leads to physical illness, a former student of mine, Susan, another United Church of Christ minister, has found greater well-being and effectiveness in claiming her vision as "God's partner in healing the world." In Susan's words this means that "I also take care of myself as well as promote healing in the church and the world. I can't be an effective healer if I am constantly stressed and fatigued." Having a vision helps Susan discern what's important and what can be left for tomorrow She reports that "each week I make a list of what needs to be done at the church and in my personal life. Because healing is important, I always include exercise, special times with my partner and children, and recreation. I also prioritize my work as a pastor. Having a vision for the day or week orders my day so that I don't do too much or too little. I recognize that unexpected things happen, and when they do, I have to revise my list but still prioritize what's important."

Having a vision helps us respond more creatively to conflict.[4] Jesus's vision statement did not immunize him from conflict. In fact, his vision of an open table and welcoming community conflicted with religious and social mores regarding cleanliness and uncleanliness. Our vision helps us recognize what is nonnegotiable in our lives and ministries. For both Stephen and Susan, having a vision means leaving some things undone to attend to "more important things," like healthy relationships and family life. Both are quite flexible in adjusting to change, but sometimes they have to say no to participation in programs that will consistently take them away from home or conflict with their physical and spiritual well-being. When conflicts occur, charting a flexible vision can guide our behaviors. The issue is not eliminating conflict in ministry; it is how we respond to conflict. Visionary thinking reminds us that while we cannot always change situations or are not fully responsible for other people's responses, we are responsible for how we respond to conflict and for preserving our integrity in times of crisis and conflict.

In the midst of dealing with conflict over the proposal that her congregation make a commitment to become "open and affirming" of gay, lesbian, transgendered, and bisexual people, Judy's commitment to a "fully inclusive ministry, reflecting Jesus's radical hospitality" required her to reach out to opponents as well as supporters of her own and the church leadership's quest to welcome diversity. Judy chose not to blame or polarize but to reach out to those who sometimes fiercely opposed her viewpoint. She invited those who disagreed with her to dinner and coffee, maintaining relationships despite differences. She continued to pastor with grace and care to supporter and opponent alike. In her own words, Judy asserted, "How can I be for radical hospitality if I ostracize those whose positions radically differ from my own?"

In dealing with conflicts regarding establishing a winter shelter at his historic church, Terry, the pastor of an urban Presbyterian congregation, felt similar to Susan. "At the heart of my understanding of ministry is the commitment 'to speak the truth with love.'" For Terry, joining truth telling with love meant "seeing God's presence in those who opposed the winter shelter, staying in fellowship with them, and addressing their concerns. It meant being mindful of my words and behavior. I constantly asked myself the question, Do I treat those who oppose me with the same care that I do those for whom I advocate? Having a vision helped Terry maintain a moral and relational compass in a time of congregational challenge. Committing ourselves to a vision doesn't always mean success, but it promotes integrity and helps us remain faithful to our calling when we might otherwise succumb to bitterness or alienation. It reminds us that maintaining our integrity and the integrity of our ministries and spiritual and relational lives is nonnegotiable, especially when we are tempted to compromise our deepest values, lash out in anger, or succumb to moral improprieties.

HEALTHY PRACTICES FOR HEALTHY PASTORS

Discovering your ministerial and personal vision is a spiritual practice. It is grounded in the process of listening to your life and then letting your life speak. You may choose to follow one of the practices—spiritual direction, clearness committee, appreciative inquiry and reflection—listed above. These are especially helpful, because they enable us to experience God's vocational voice moving within the many voices of our lives. In the spirit of psychiatrist and spiritual guide Gerald May, as Kate Epperly and I describe in *Tending to the Holy*, we need to pause, notice, open, stretch, and respond to God's presence within our gifts, experiences, and encounters. Habakkuk reminds us that we need to write our vision down so that it will be an easily remembered guidepost for our personal and professional lives. Three practices help ground and shape your vision over time and circumstance: the use of a visionary affirmation, praying your affirmation, and daily spiritual examination.

Visionary Affirmation

In articulating a visionary affirmation, you create a phrase or word that you can repeat regularly and that reminds you of your personal and professional mission. For example, Jesus's words from John 10:10 can be stated in terms of a visionary affirmation: "I share God's abundant life with everyone I encounter." Jesus's proclamation from Mark 1 can be transformed into the following affirmation: "God is near and I share God's message of good news." My own personal vision might be transformed into a brief affirmation: "I bring beauty and blessing to everyone I meet."

After you have formulated a personal and professional vision, based on your experience of God's presence in your life in light of your gifts, circumstances, and experience, prayerfully discern how you might describe your vision in one sentence. Use your affirmative vision as a reminder and guidepost in the course of your day.

Praying Your Visionary Affirmation

Repeating your affirmation throughout the day can become a prayer word for you. Praying your affirmation can be integrated with prayers of thanksgiving and petition, such as "I thank you, God, for calling me to be a blessing in this situation." Or, "God, help me bring beauty and blessing to this situation." If your aim involves radical hospitality, your prayer might be "Help me, O God, to be hospitable and welcoming in this situation." Or it might be, "Thank you for making me a channel of radical hospitality to friend and opponent alike." Praying our affirmations keeps us connected to the wellspring of energy and inspiration. We are not alone in personal and professional vocations but are always supported by a companioning God.

Spiritual Examination

Spiritual examination is a contemporary approach to the daily examen, pioneered by Ignatius of Loyola. It involves a prayerful reflection on your day, simply noticing, without judgment, whether you have been attentive to your personal and professional vision or visions. At the end of each day, you may choose to find a comfortable place for five to ten minutes to examine your day using the following guides:

> Give thanks for the gift of life and vision.
> Reflect on the events of your day.
> Contemplate your nearness or distance from God and your vision throughout the day
> Meditate on a particular moment in the day as a window into your spiritual life: In that moment, where did you experience God? In what ways were you guided by your vision? What feelings were evoked? How did your response mirror your overall spiritual well-being?
> Place that event and your whole day in God's care.
> Conclude with gratitude for the day and prayers for tomorrow.

10

EMBRACING GRIEF

But we do not want you to be uninformed, brothers and sisters,
about those who have died, so that you may not grieve as others do
who have no hope.

—1 Thessalonians 4:13

The hand of the LORD came upon me, and he brought me out by the
spirit of the LORD and set me down in the middle of a valley; it was
full of bones. He led me all around them; there were very many lying
in the valley, and they were very dry. He said to me, "Mortal, can
these bones live?" I answered, "O Lord GOD, you know." Then he
said to me, "Prophesy to these bones, and say to them: O dry bones,
hear the word of the LORD. Thus says the Lord GOD to these bones: I
will cause breath to enter you, and you shall live. I will lay sinews on
you, and will cause flesh to come upon you, and cover you with skin,
and put breath in you, and you shall live. . . . And you shall know that
I am the LORD."

—Ezekiel 37:1–5, 6

THE UNIVERSALITY OF GRIEF

One of my favorite spiritual sayings is attributed to the Protestant
reformer Martin Luther, who observed that in the midst of life, we are
surrounded by death; and in the midst of death, we are surrounded by
life. The realities of death and loss can destroy us or provide pathways
to spiritual transformation and enlightenment. The story is told of a

young Indian prince Gautama whose father sought to shelter him from the sorrows of life. He lived a life of luxury, surrounded by youth and beauty until he ventured forth from the palace on three successive days, during which he encountered an aged man, a sick person, and a corpse. The young prince was shaken to his core and began to ponder the transitory nature of life. On the fourth day Gautama continued his spiritual adventure, this time synchronously encountering a monk whose vocation inspired the future Enlightened One to leave the palace on a quest for spiritual wholeness in a world of suffering and death.

While Christian spiritual leaders may wish to elaborate on Gautama Buddha's judgment that "life is suffering" in light of the realities of creation as God's blessing and resurrection as God's transformation, the encounter with death has always been an invitation to spiritual leadership among our shamanic, prophetic, and monastic spiritual predecessors. Today, if you ask a group of pastors about their life experiences, many will respond that pivotal in their vocational call were experiences with death that led them to embark on a quest for healing. Death colors ministry, and as one experienced pastor remarked, "I think all ministry involves some form of grief work." I recall the surprise of one seminarian who related, "I never thought ministry had so much to do with death. My field education supervising pastor seems to be dealing with death and the possibility of death all the time. Each week he's visiting the hospital, the nursing facility, hospice, and the Alzheimer's unit. He always seems to be comforting the bereaved and conducting a funeral. I don't know if I have the stamina for this kind of work."

Death has many faces, which shape the reality of grief in our time. This text is the result of some thirty years of reflection on the spirituality of the traditional professions—priesthood, law, and medicine. I began studying professional wellness, working with physicians and medical students, when I served as Senior Protestant Chaplain at Georgetown University. I found that unresolved grief was a source of stress and substance abuse among medical professionals. Years later I worked with overwhelmed and overstressed law students and lawyers, inviting them to explore healthy approaches to balancing personal, professional, and relational demands in practicing law.[1]

I believe that today's pastors also need to find creative ways to respond to the emotional, spiritual, and physical stresses that accompany their priestly vocation. For pastors, grief is a daily reality. Beyond the obvious grief-producing situations—death of beloved congregants and tragic deaths of children—pastors deal with many subtle and often unacknowledged forms of grief. These include the radical changes in North American culture, the death of Christendom and the decline of the influence of Christianity in the larger society, membership losses, moving from one congregation to another, death of spouses and relational losses, people leaving the church for theological reasons or to attend larger, "more vital" congregations, a sense of failure and professional disillusionment, and the diminishment of the minister's social influence. All these are signs of the transitory and precarious nature of everything we love as well as the pain that ensues when we try to hold on to stability in a world of flux. Life is change, and change involves loss as well as creative transformation.

THE INESCAPABILITY OF GRIEF

In the course of writing this book, one of my primary sources of wisdom came from the experiences of pastors who shared their stories through conversations, Internet messages, and Facebook messages and responses. As I began drafting each chapter, I would ask my Facebook and face-to-face friends a question related to the theme. By far, the issue of loss and grief elicited the greatest number of responses. It is clear that grief is pervasive in ministry. Pastors grieve their own personal losses (divorce, death of a spouse, death of parents, leaving home if they are young adults entering ministry), the disestablishment of Christianity from the forefront of North American life, the loss of membership, broken dreams and the loss of ministerial idealism, leaving a beloved congregation or being forced out of a position, and the losses occasioned by retirement. In the following paragraphs, I will let these pastors speak in their own words. Their comments are impressionistic and experiential rather than clinical. In their concreteness, they reflect the grief that most pastors feel at some point in their vocational life. Perhaps you will recognize your own experiences of grief and loss as you reflect on their experiences. You may also experience new hope and a sense of healing as your own experiences are mirrored by others.

Catherine, a United Methodist pastor in North Carolina, recalls the challenges of her first pastorate. "Like many new pastors in the Methodist system, I was given three churches to pastor. In my first six months, there were several deaths and a number of life-threatening illnesses among my parishioners, and I was feeling overwhelmed with death and grief. I didn't have time to process my feelings. I had forgotten to keep passing it all on to the Lord. It was very difficult to find my way through all the suffering, but God is so good and so faithful, and despite being overwhelmed emotionally, I grew as a person and pastor in this difficult time."

A Lutheran pastor in rural Minnesota, Matt received a call from a grieving family as the movers were unloading his furniture at the parsonage. "I had the 'perfect storm' death the first month. It seemed like they were all waiting for the settled pastor to come. I had nine deaths. I didn't know whether I was coming or going, and even ended up at the wrong funeral home on one occasion. Luckily, the right place was only five miles farther down the road. I wouldn't have gotten through it without the emotional support of my wife, a seminary mentor, and long runs on the country roads. Sometimes my salvation those first few weeks was the odd combination of morning prayer and coming home Fridays for pizza, beer, and a video just to let go of the pain I felt."

Pastors also struggle with death and illness in their own families. When our son Matt was diagnosed with a rare form of cancer, I was devastated. "This isn't the way it's supposed to be. He should be taking care of me, rather than me accompanying my once healthy and muscular six-foot-two-inch son to chemotherapy." Needless to say, I was emotionally and spiritually drained. I will always be grateful to Riess Potterveld, former president of Lancaster Theological Seminary, and the leadership team of Disciples United Community Church for giving Kate and me the space to be with our son in Washington, DC, a hundred miles away from our home in Lancaster, during the three months of his chemotherapy treatment. They assured me that I needed to put my family first and family responsibilities were essential to my academic and pastoral vocations. I wouldn't have made it through this crisis apart from a commitment to daily meditation, walking prayer, and exercise; the support of a few good friends; and the companionship of my wife, Kate. I am pleased to say that my son is now five years cancer-free and the father of two young sons! I am grateful to friends, physicians, pharmaceuticals, and God for his recovery and my ability to grow as a pastor from this experience.

Jim, an Episcopalian pastor, recalls how difficult it was to do his first funeral following his grandfather's death. "I had to take a lot of time for prayer beforehand and breathe deeply throughout the service. I was stretched and felt weak, but now I know what Paul meant when he affirmed that in weakness he is strong and that God's grace is sufficient for us."

A former student, Patricia, reflects on her experience of the death of her husband: "Having just lost my husband, I have found that some people find it difficult to reach out to clergy because they are supposed to have these issues 'nipped in the bud' and can deal with them better than everyone else. That certainly isn't the case. We need TLC too, and I am appreciative of the TLC I have received." Patricia's comments remind me of a plaque at a major Paris hospital. While it is intended for physicians and nurses, it applies to pastors as well: "We are the dying taking care of the dying." We are all touched by death, and how we respond to death and grief—our own and our congregants and loved ones—can enrich and enlighten or diminish and depress.

Pastors experience the death of relationships. A Metropolitan Community Church pastor, Pam identifies the breakup with her partner with her departure from one of her congregations. "I just couldn't handle the emotional stress of dealing with my emotional devastation and the neediness of my transitional urban congregation. I had to take some time off, recover, and get counseling. I came to the conclusion that I needed to seek out a less demanding community at least for the short term, and I was able to find a call as interim pastor of a healthy, stable congregation. This gave me the time I needed to recover." Sid felt the same way after he and his wife broke up, leaving him with primary custody of his three preteen children. A United Church of Christ pastor, Sid recalls, "I didn't know how I would make it, but the support of my conference minister and the understanding of my church helped me find the inner and outer resources to face my loss and sense of failure. They reflected back to me the grace I'd preached to them. It took a while to recover, and I needed to refer congregants with relational issues to a local colleague, but with time and therapy and the understanding of others, I am now emotionally sound and ready to balance my ministry and parenting in healthy ways."

Moving is one of life's most stressful experiences. Can you imagine how Abraham and Sarah felt when God called them to go from their familiar place to the promised land of their future? I suspect that they looked back longingly and wondered why they chose to follow God's calling. Pastors often leave congregations with whom they have pastored with love and excellence. Cecilia tells of the pain she felt after leaving her Western Massachusetts Unitarian Universalist congregation to accept a call near Boston. "I felt that it was time to go after ten years, and the future beckoned me forward. I knew that the new church needed my gifts and would help me grow. But how I cried when I drove off for final time! I already missed these people! I held my tears back during the final worship service, but I was a fountain afterward. I would continue to love these people and would encounter them in the future, but they would no longer be my congregants. I would miss their faces, words, and even their peculiarities."

Samuel cried in both despair and relief when he left a contentious International Council of Community Churches congregation. "I left before I was pushed, but it was still hard. I felt like a failure and unworthy to pastor a church. I'm in a good place emotionally and vocationally now. But I grieve my inability to succeed there and the lost opportunities to do good ministry. I had to go, but it is still painful to remember. I'm in a good place now, but it took the help of a clergy support group and some loving colleagues to renew my faith in myself and my ministry."

Moving is not easy for younger pastors either. Many have always lived in home or academic settings, such as dormitories and seminary apartments. Now they may have to move hundreds or even thousands of miles from home to set up their first household, as single or married. A midwestern American Baptist pastor, Sterling was excited about his first call to be an associate minister of a New England congregation, but he also felt the loss of the Indiana home in which he grew up and the midwestern schools he attended. "I'm really looking forward to living near Boston—to the museums, artistic life, seacoast, and schools, but it's so far from home. I'll miss regular outings with my sister and my folks. It will be hard, but God's future beckons."

Retirement is a significant source of grief among many pastors. It also touches their partners and spouses. Retirement means a change in vocational status, daily routine, and relationships. It also signals the beginning of a number of necessary losses that accompany even a healthy aging process. David notes that "I didn't know what to do the first month after I retired. I had so much energy and so many good ideas and didn't know where to use them. My wife and I grieved a lot at first. Though we were excited about living near our children and grandchildren, we missed our home and yard and the friends we'd made. My wife missed the women's fellowship and choir, two of her most sustaining groups of friends. We knew we had to maintain appropriate boundaries, but the letting go was painful."

Andrew speaks of retirement as "being put out to pasture and marginalized after being at the center of things." He also questions the absolutism that is often implied in boundary and interim ministry training. "The judicatory official and interim minister treated me like I was an accident waiting to happen. They told me in no uncertain terms that I was to stay away from church, even if a former member asked me to participate in a funeral. They didn't even want me to attend! I felt utterly abandoned and judged as an offender, even though I had a forty-year, unblemished record as a pastor."

Given the interdependent nature of life, understandings of absolute boundaries need to be reimagined in more holistic ways. Traditional boundary training follows both a dualistic and a pathological model, assuming that relationships with former pastors are always trouble and that people can be uprooted completely from professional and personal relationships without serious emotional and spiritual harm being done. I believe a more self-aware and health-oriented approach to boundaries would assume appropriate ongoing relationships, even at rites of passages such as funerals and weddings, while preserving the integrity of the current pastor's spiritual leadership and the need for the congregation to move on. This relational approach to boundaries requires a good deal of intentionality, but practiced wisely it is healthy for pastors and congregations alike.

A major area of grief many pastors face is the reality of membership losses, whether due to death, moving, dissatisfaction, or changing communities. As she considered her inner-city Presbyterian church, Sandy lamented, "I feel so sad when a member dies or moves away, not to mention when I experience a once-vital leader experiencing the ravages of aging and debilitation. You invest yourself in people, and though I have to let go, it still hurts." A Lutheran pastor in a dying Dakota town, Steve added, "It's especially tough when people leave because of some lack in the church—either the church isn't lively enough in worship, hasn't a children's program, or lacks a praise band or big screen in worship. People are moving away from town, and those who stay are driving twenty miles to stop at Walmart and go to bigger churches. I feel like I've failed somehow, even though I rationally recognize that our little church can't do everything and our town has half the population it did twenty years ago." A suburban United Church of Christ pastor, Sarah felt the pain of ten families departing as a result of her denomination's support of marriage equality and ordination of openly gay and lesbian pastors. "It couldn't be helped, but I feel the void of their absence. They were good people and active in the church. But they just couldn't live with our church's stand on homosexuality. Though I disagreed with them, it was hard to see them go."

Pastors share the same feelings of grief related to membership loss that their congregants feel, many of whom are depressed at their congregation's consistent loss of membership and who long for the "good old days" when the pews were filled and children bounded up the aisle for the children's sermon. We have been told that membership growth is a sure sign of pastoral excellence and professional skills, but often churches decline numerically as a result of factors beyond the pastor's control, such as changing neighborhoods, population and economic decline, and changes in the surrounding spiritual culture.

One rather recent source of grief is the displacement of Christianity and the end of Christendom. The mainline has become the old line, and even evangelical churches are losing their place in the center channels of Christianity. The church is at the periphery of people's lives. In fact, there are hundreds of spiritual options as well as the choice to be "none of the above." Many people live in denial of the loss of Christendom or fight it tooth and nail, hoping to reinstitute America as a Christian nation with biblical values regarding marriage, sexuality, and birth control. But, as one pastor says, "the grief of this loss is enormous. It calls into question our whole way of life, our theology, our sacraments, and our God, if our Christian faith is just one of many. What's worse for me is that many of my congregants' children can live quite well without the church. In fact, the church is irrelevant to their lives, except for baptisms and Christmas. The Easter Sunday celebration doesn't even bring them back to church anymore. I feel a lot like the technician in the old Maytag commercial. There's nothing for me to do most of the time in the community, and folks call me only when they need a wedding or funeral."

Singer-songwriter Bob Dylan once asserted that "the times they are a changin'" and that we'd better get used to it or we'll be left behind. Near retirement, Gregg, a Cooperative Baptist pastor, laments the changes the past forty years have brought to the way people see his ministry. "Once upon a time I was somebody. Being a pastor commanded respect and a central place in the community's life. But now in this post-Christian time, most people don't have a clue about what I do. They see pastors as innocuous figures performing weddings on television or in the movies or as nincompoops burning the Quran, picketing military funerals, or opposing science in schools. I feel like I have to explain myself or distinguish myself from the public perception all the time." Marilyn, now beginning her thirtieth year of ministry in the Episcopal Church, grieves the loss of youth in church. "The myth used to be that they come back when they have children, but that happens less and less these days. I feel bittersweet on Christmas when I see some of my confirmands and their spouses and children and know that they have better things to do than go to church on Sunday mornings. Sleeping late, soccer practice, or the irrelevance of our programs to their lives keeps them away, and that hurts. It also hurts that this parish won't adapt to the changed world and change its worship style and time to welcome the young adults and their children."

GRIEVING WITH HOPE

Unresolved grief can be debilitating. It can lead to depression, illness, substance abuse, and compassion fatigue. It can also challenge our sense of vocation. Grieving with hope is a matter of theology and community. It takes a village to raise a child, train a pastor, and insure pastoral well-being and excellence over the long haul. In this case, the village is a network of supportive relationships that allow pastors, like the psalmist, to explore the full range of emotions that attend grief and loss.

Hope is embodied theology. It emerges with and shapes our theological visions. In reflecting on her ongoing recovery from leaving a turbulent congregation, Susan, recently called to a Lutheran congregation on the East Coast, found the words from Romans 8 central to her well-being. "I lived with two phrases: 'In all things God works for good' and 'Nothing can separate me from the love of God.' I didn't see them as magic but as promises that God was with me in my pain and that God would never abandon me. These scriptures helped me stay open to possibilities for healing in my personal and professional life."

During my son's cancer, I prayed the Jesus Prayer as I took my predawn walk in the vicinity of Georgetown University Hospital where he was a patient. I cried out in my anguish, "Lord, have mercy. Christ, have mercy. Lord, have mercy." As he began to recover and health was on the horizon, I added the hymn I learned in my childhood Baptist church:

> Great is thy faithfulness, O dear Creator,
> There is no shadow of turning in thee. . . .
> Great is thy faithfulness, great is thy faithfulness,
> Morning by morning new mercies I see.
> All I have needed thy hand hath provided.
> Great is thy faithfulness, God unto me. [2]

Healthy theology in times of grief proclaims that God is with us, feeling our pain, grief, and sense of failure and providing new possibilities—resurrection hopes—in times of loss. Healthy theology does not promise success in every endeavor, perfect health, and congregational growth; it does assure us of God's loving presence, even when God appears most absent. God's still small voice is speaking in the depths of our hearts, and God's loving creativity emerges in new insights, surprising energy, loving friends, and synchronous encounters.

The word is made flesh and is revealed in God's presence among us, not only in the life of Jesus but also in the encouragement of loving companions. Sally admits gratefully, "I couldn't do it alone. I couldn't face tomorrow after my divorce without a fellowship of colleagues and friends who called me, restored my spirits, and gave encouragement on lonely nights. I also found a trusted counselor who helped me face my pain and discover daylight on the other side. In the darkness I saw a light; and it was God crying along with me and showing me the way to the future."

Other pastors find hope in spiritual direction. When Doug realized that his feelings of failure over membership losses in his Disciples of

Christ congregation were undermining the quality of his pastoral leadership, he sought out a wise and compassionate spiritual director with whom he has now met monthly for three years. "I take my sorrow and joy to him. In his care and gentle questions I discover that I am not alone nor am I fully responsible for my congregation's decline. He helps me put things in perspective and enables me to discover that I can still creatively and faithfully pastor a numerically declining congregation. He keeps reminding me of Jesus's own failures to gather a large following. He often asks, 'Do you think you need to be more successful than Jesus?' and that helps me run the race with hope and energy, knowing that Jesus felt the same way I do and that he persevered by placing his life in God's care."

Spiritual growth and pastoral colleague groups also enable ministers to deal with the pain of loss and grief. In the company of colleagues, we discover that we are not alone and find ways to cope with feelings of grief and failure. Extroverted in spirit, Episcopalian priest Peter found his ecumenical colleague group helpful in understanding the dynamics of pluralism and postmodernism. "I thought my church was unique, but in hearing the stories of colleagues and sharing my own, I discovered that we are part of changes in culture and spirituality that are shaping ministry and congregational life in new ways. I didn't initially have the tools to face these changes creatively, but as we work things out in our monthly meetings, I am finding ways to help my congregation understand what's going on and to explore new ways to address seekers, the self-described 'none of the above,' and the spiritual-but-not-religious folk. I'm not so desperate anymore."

We can grieve with hope because of healthy relationships that sustain us: a vision of God as the fellow sufferer who understands, the touch of a friend, the wisdom of colleagues, and the space for anguish and insight created by counselors and spiritual directors. The pain can be great, and we may need to seek therapeutic and medicinal support. Depending on others—including mental health professionals and medication—is a sign of wisdom and hope, not weakness, as we seek excellence in our ministerial leadership. We are not alone. God's sustaining and creative love upholds us and is mediated to us through moments of divine companionship and the embodied friendship of companions, colleagues, and professionals. Thanks be to God!

HEALTHY PRACTICES FOR HEALTHY PASTORS

Responding to the many faces of personal and corporate grief requires us to join solitude and community. We need time to adjust our emotional and spiritual aspects to the reality of loss. We also need a community of trusted friends to provide support and counsel when we face personal and institutional losses.

Growing in Spiritual and Emotional Stature

One of my graduate school professors, Bernard Loomer, saw stature or size as a primary spiritual virtue. Being a person of stature involves having a spirit large enough to embrace a significant range of spiritual, intellectual, and emotional experiences. When it comes to responding to grief, a person of stature seeks to embrace a full range of feelings while still preserving her or his spiritual center. The first practice is a meditation based on Loomer's concept of stature. Take a few minutes to reflect on Loomer's words:

> By size I mean the stature of [your] soul, the range and depth of [your] love, [your] capacity for relationships. I mean the volume of life you can take into your being and still maintain your integrity and individuality, the intensity and variety of outlook you can entertain in the unity of your being without feeling defensive or insecure. I mean the strength of your spirit to encourage others to become freer in the development of their diversity and uniqueness. I mean the power to sustain more complex and enriching tensions. I mean the magnanimity of concern to provide conditions that enable others to increase in stature.[3]

Take fifteen or twenty minutes today and over the next few days to reflect on your current experiences of grief. This is not so much an analytic experience but a spiritual examination of your emotional and relational life. In a prayerful spirit, consider the following questions. You might even think of them as a conversation with God about your current ministerial and personal life.

What are the most significant losses you have experienced in the past year?

Are any of these experiences of loss chronic, that is, ongoing in
nature? For example, slow but consistent congregational membership loss, a sense of irrelevance to the larger culture, a sense
of uncertainty about your professional life, a chronic ailment or
physical diminishment.

How many family members, relatives, or close friends have faced
critical illness or died in the past year?

How many family members, relatives, or close friends have experienced serious illnesses of body, mind, or spirit?

How would you describe your emotional response to these losses?

Have these losses affected your personal relationships in any way?

Have these losses affected your professional relationships and sense
of vocation in any way?

Where do you need to seek healing in relationship to these losses?

Where do you experience God in your experiences of grief and loss?

Set aside some time for journaling or drawing your losses. If it is more
helpful for your growth, you may also write a poem or song.

Surround this time of reflection with prayer. You might choose a
psalm (Psalm 22, 23, 46, 91, 139) as a source of inspiration. The beauty
of the Psalms is that they encompass the totality of life. Nothing is
withheld from God—elation and desolation, celebration and grief, companionship and abandonment, friendship and loneliness, praise and despair. As another Baptist song of my childhood affirms, you can "take it
to the Lord in prayer."

If you find yourself discovering an all-pervasive sadness, grief, or
depression, I encourage you to contact your family physician, a counselor familiar and appreciative of spirituality and ministry, or a mental
health professional who is able to prescribe appropriate medication.

Circles of Healing

Every communion Sunday, my childhood Baptist church concluded the
service by singing, "Blest be the ties that bind our hearts in Christian
love; The fellowship of kindred minds is like to that above."[4] We need a
fellowship of kindred spirits—what Carrie Newcomer calls "a gathering
of spirits"—to help us experience God's embodied and incarnational
movements toward hope and healing. Henri Nouwen appropriately

notes, "No one person can fulfil all your needs. But the community can truly hold you. The community can let you experience the fact that, beyond your anguish, there are human hands that hold you and show you God's faithful love."[5]

In the company of people who share your experiences, you can sense God's healing presence and discover unexpected pathways to the future when you thought there was no way forward. Accordingly, many pastors have found healing and wholeness through colleague groups whose primary purpose is to support each other, edify each other's ministries, and share each other's joys and sorrows. In such groups, you give and receive. You also discover that you are not alone in your sense of loss. You can also receive practical advice on how to respond to funerals, congregational grief, weariness from the "perfect storm" of congregational losses, and maintaining your own well-being in the face of the burdens of death and grief. Within colleague groups, you discover that as we support the healing of others, we experience greater energy and wellness. As the biblical tradition affirms, giving and receiving are united in promoting the well-being of everyone, including you. In your love and care for others, you can awaken to a relational healing in which God's healing energies flow through your life and enrich everyone you meet.

11

HEALTHY RELATIONSHIPS

For just as the body is one and has many members, and all the members of the body, though many, are one body, so it is with Christ. . . . If one member suffers, all suffer together with it; if one member is honored, all rejoice together with it. Now you are the body of Christ and individually members of it.

—1 Corinthians 12:12, 26–27

Set me as a seal upon your heart, as a seal upon your arm; for love is strong as death.

—Song of Songs 8:6

MINISTRY IN AN INTERDEPENDENT UNIVERSE

The biblical tradition is relational in nature, and so is the vocation of spiritual leadership. Though we seldom receive the whole story of any biblical character's life, we can imagine the intimacy of Abraham and Sarah as they set out as senior adults on a journey toward an unknown horizon; we can experience the love between Ruth and Naomi that inspired Ruth to risk immigrating to a strange land; we can affirm the intimate love of Jonathan and David for each other and feel David's pain at Jonathan's death; we are grateful for the loving care and honesty of Mordecai in his role as Esther's spiritual advisor and for Esther's willingness to trust the wisdom of his counsel. Jesus's ministry was centered on relationships: you can feel his affection for Peter and the

Zebedee brothers; his love for Lazarus, Mary, and Martha; his spiritual relationship with Mary of Magdala; the transforming power of table fellowship with outcasts; the power of his loving healing touch; and his pain at Judas's betrayal.

Plato once noted that a philosopher without love is dead. Echoing Plato, the apostle Paul proclaims that love fulfills and gives meaning to our spiritual gifts. Without the mutuality of love in the body of Christ, our greatest gifts amount to nothing. Relationship is at the heart of ministry: we may not always like specific congregants, but our quest to love them is essential to our well-being and effectiveness as pastors and to our ability to bring out the best in our partnerships with our congregants. Emphasis on boundary training in ministry is not about legalism or one-size-fits-all approaches to ministerial relationships; rather, awareness of appropriate boundaries enables us love rightly in our personal and professional lives. Regardless of the theme, this book has ultimately been about relationships: healthy ministry begins with loving God, ourselves, and others in ways that bring beauty and justice to the world and those who are in our personal and professional care. In this chapter we will be reflecting on the importance of a pastor's relationships with friends, family, spouses, and partners. Healthy relationships beyond the church are essential to overall personal well-being and professional integrity. Still, many pastors struggle to find time, energy, and emotional intimacy in their closest relationships. The urgency of the moment and apparently important priorities of day-to-day ministry often crowd out both quantity and quality time with those who most depend on our love. Healthy relationships are possible in ministry. It is, like everything else in healthy ministry, a matter of intentionality and mindfulness.

CHALLENGING RELATIONSHIPS

Ministry is profoundly relational, and the quality of our relationships profoundly shapes our ministry. The flexibility of ministry can be a challenge as well as a gift, and our marital status can bring joy or sorrow to our ministerial lives.

The Ambiguity of Flexibility

A minister's schedule is primarily discretionary in nature. The essential and nonnegotiable events of congregational ministry—preaching, meetings, Christian formation—occur within a parameter of about ten scheduled hours each week. The rest of a pastor's week is determined by priorities, choice, and happenstance. As I noted earlier, we can't manage time, but we can be intentional about when and where we work after we've "paid the rent" by leading worship and fulfilling responsibilities at other scheduled events. The good news is that pastors can choose times to be with our families or to cultivate hobbies and relationships or to focus on continuing education. Throughout my professional life, I have been an early riser. I have already described how I do virtually all my writing, sermon preparation, and study before nine o'clock. Proof is this morning's writing: it is 5:00 a.m. in Washington, DC, and the streets of my urban neighborhood are silent. Yet here I am spending the hour writing in between morning prayer and meditation and my first walk of the day. I want to accomplish some of my professional tasks before I leave at 10:00 a.m. to go to a children's play, Winnie the Pooh, with my son and oldest grandson. A prolific writer, I have on more than one occasion assured congregations during the course of interviews that by the time most of them begin their work day, I have been writing, studying, and planning for nearly three hours.

In contrast, Stewart is a night person. He comes home most days at 3:30 p.m. to play with his children, and on evenings when he doesn't have meetings, after getting the children ready for bed he spends time watching television and talking with his wife or reading a book. He does his sermon preparation and study most evenings between 11:00 p.m. and 1:00 a.m. and begins his work day at 10:00 a.m. after the kids have gone to school. An Episcopalian priest, Stewart is always prepared and effective in his leadership of a growing midsized congregation. As he says, "The flexibility of ministry has given the best of all possible worlds. I can spend time with my family, while giving the church what it needs daily and weekly in terms of pastoral leadership."

For other pastors, the flexibility of ministry is a real challenge to personal self-care and family life. Adam, a Metropolitan Community Church pastor, says, "No one ever blows the whistle on ministry. The work is never done, and I have trouble quitting. My spouse regularly complains that I'm at work even when I'm home, making phone calls, writing e-mails, and responding to text messages. Sometimes I wish I had a nine-to-five job with a clearly defined schedule. But that's not ministry."

Ministry is always implicitly twenty-four/seven, regardless of our intentionality. Another Metropolitan Community Church pastor, Ruth, notes, "You can't schedule emergencies. While not everything is urgent, on more than one occasion I've had to get up from the dinner table or miss one of my kids' games when the call came about a congregant's death or a car accident involving teenagers from our small town. Still, a lot of calls can wait, and I try to make dinnertimes and family evenings at home sacred. Even Jesus spent times with friends and took time off the job for his prayer life. If Jesus can do it, so can I."

As you reflect on the stories of Ruth, Stewart, Adam, and me, consider your own approach to the flexibility of ministry. Do you use your time wisely so that you can have more flexibility for family, self-care, and spiritual nurture? While some weeks are nonstop, especially around Holy Week, Easter, and Christmas or when a member dies or a community tragedy occurs, most weeks are fairly routine, and some are, frankly, easy. Do you take advantage of low-demand weeks to get ahead on your studies, to go to a film with your spouse or partner, to go on a hike, or to play with your children? Do you take time each day to nurture your loved ones, care for yourself, and grow in the arts of ministry?

The Joys and Challenges of Family Life

One thing I've discovered in the course of writing a book on clergy self-care and well-being is that each chapter could be extended into a small book. I've had to be selective about the issues addressed in this and every chapter. As a child of a small-town pastor, I know firsthand the challenges of ministers' families: feeling like you're in a fishbowl, and even though you're just a kid, held up as an example, good or bad, for other children; being subject to small town gossip or hearing inadvertently complaints about your pastor-parent; having your parent jump up from the dinner table in response to an emergency. But there were also joys: my dad and I read together every morning; I had the run of the church as a second home and playground; my dad would come home afternoons to see me play baseball or to play catch with me in the backyard. On balance, I am grateful for my life as a child of the manse, but my gratitude is mixed with memories about church controversies and the insecurity of a small-town pastor's life. I vowed never to become a pastor, and yet I am called to be a teaching pastor, committed to congregational life and to supporting pastors and congregations in their quest for excellent and life-supporting ministry.

For many married as well as single pastors the fishbowl nature of ministry is a challenge, especially when the parsonage is next door or the congregation is in a rural or small-town setting. One single-parent pastor was surprised on a Saturday morning to find five trustees working in her basement. She now can laughingly relate the story: "No one told me they'd be changing the water heater I'd been complaining about. When I heard their banging around, they're lucky I didn't come downstairs with a shotgun or in a skimpy nightgown!" Needless to say, after she explained to them the nature of boundaries, they haven't come unannounced since. "I suspect," she continues, "their wives gave them an earful when they heard about their husbands' social blunder."

Due to the economic recession of the past five years, many pastors and their families have struggled to make ends meet and often go without cost-of-living increases or face cuts in benefits and salary. Economic issues are especially difficult in small-town congregations where the pastor's spouse may have difficulty finding work, or when a pastor has moved across the country to an expensive urban area and discovered what looked like a great salary just barely pays the bills until her or his spouse or partner finds employment. Although the situation is changing, ministers' wives in particular have dealt regularly with the ambiguity of being considered an unpaid employee of the congregation. In some churches they are expected to host visitors, go on calls with their husbands, take significant roles in Christian education and vacation church school, and be involved in congregational problem solving. Most pastors' wives want to support their husbands, but many of them also have employment outside the home or are raising young children. These same implicit demands are seldom made of male spouses. During times when my primary employment was teaching, chaplaincy, and administration, congregants made virtually no demands of me as my wife's ministerial spouse. I showed up at the men's fellowship and on work days at church to support my wife's ministry, but never because I felt I had to be there. Thankfully, even in small-town congregations, pastors' wives are now being seen as interdependent but unique individuals with lives outside the church.

In the words of one married pastor, echoing the sentiments of many of her peers, "Boundaries are everything in finding a healthy balance between ministry and family. I have found that I need to be very intentional about my schedule to preserve time for family and friends. I have to say no to requests from denominational officials and make it clear that my family is a priority along with my ministry. At first this was a challenge for me—especially as a woman—to be assertive without being perceived as aggressive. But I found a gentle way of reminding my congregants that I can't be a good pastor without being a good wife and mother, and now they get it." Steve adds, "I think it's easier for a man to express boundaries in church than a woman. I wish it were different, but the people in my church, especially the women, see my parenting and time with my wife as a model for their own husbands. I'm not sure I like being a model held up to the husbands of the church, and I'm not sure the husbands like it either! But I've made it clear that I'll be there in emergencies and that I work hard to grow this church and provide good pastoral care. I also give the same attention to my family. I want my work as a pastor to bring joy to their lives too!"

The Joys and Challenges of Single Pastors

Being single in ministry can lead to feelings of loneliness or freedom. I recall a Jesuit priest who once observed, "It must be difficult to be married and be a minister. I can't imagine functioning as a priest if I also had to respond to all the demands of family life and marriage." A happily single pastor once shared, "I am glad to be free to lead my life as I want to. I can be a pastor without guilt, responding to whatever comes my way without having to worry about its impact on others, and I can also pretty much determine my schedule without having to meet others' expectations."

Still, single pastors face unique challenges in their quest for wholeness in ministry. Charles describes his experience as a single pastor by the phrase "very difficult and lonely." He recalls with a degree of humor all the times people tried to set him up on dates with their daughters or friends at work and is grateful that he finally found someone outside the church with whom to share his life. Delores asserts, "Being a single pastor is very difficult. I have trouble explaining who I am to others. Some people think I'm a lesbian. I'm not, not that there's anything wrong with that, but I don't like that that's where people go. I have tried online dating and found that I got matched with men who were looking for a stay-at-home mommy, and that's not my call in my life, so that didn't work out. In trying to date, I spent a lot of time explaining the difference between a nun and a female pastor. Sometimes I ended up listening to confessions, and that never went anywhere. A lot of well-meaning church ladies tried setting me up with co-workers and friends, but that never worked well either."

Many married pastors object to the phrase "two for the price of one" in describing the role of their spouses. Single pastors face a corresponding dilemma. Whereas some congregants have some appreciation for the time limitations and boundaries built into marriage and family life, many congregants believe that single pastors don't have a life outside the church and are always available for meetings and church activities. In reflecting on some of the challenges he's faced as a single pastor, Donald asserts that not having a relational partner can lead to misunderstandings about the quality of a single pastor's effectiveness: "I think a big issue for the single pastor is that whatever church he or she is serving has likely always had married pastors and has become accustomed to the spouses being full-time or part-time volunteers, so people wonder why the single man or woman doesn't seem to be getting as much done as the previous ones. And a failure to recognize that the single pastor doesn't have someone at home to help pick up some of the slack in cooking, doing dishes and laundry, cleaning, running errands, grocery shopping, and so on. You're on your own with no support when you're single in ministry!"

Edwin notes the impact of the bias toward marriage in the relationships of single pastors and congregants: "If a married pastor says to the church, 'I can't meet that night, my kid has a basketball game or a play' or 'My wife and I have a date night planned' or 'I need to take the afternoon off to take my wife to a doctor's appointment,' that is understood—but if the single man or woman says, 'I can't meet that night, I have plans with friends' or 'I can't do anything that afternoon because I have a doctor's appointment,' they are often met with the request, 'Why can't you reschedule it?' There is a sense that the single person, being single, has a calendar that is always up for modification, because there is never anything really important on it. That simply isn't true—sometimes it takes weeks to find the right time to get together with friends or to schedule a medical appointment."

Sheila notes a disparity in the treatment of single men and single women in ministry. "In my experience, single, male pastors are treated like princes of the church. People bring single guys pies and casseroles. Even married pastors, in small town America, have dinners brought over when their wives are out of town. This is not the case for women whose husbands are out of town." But I've known a few single, male pastors who hide upstairs when they see a well-meaning matron, casserole or pie in hand, heading toward the front door. Tired from a day's work, they don't want to pay the price of a long conversation in return for a good meal.

Virtually every small-town or rural single pastor with whom I've corresponded shared some version of the following lament: "It's like being in a fishbowl. People are interested in my social life and regularly comment about it. I'd go crazy if I didn't have friends and family I can see on a regular basis." Today many newly ordained pastors are single, and whether they are young or in midlife, their first congregational call is often in a remote setting. As Veronica, a small-town United Methodist pastor noted, speaking for many others, "It's tough being out in the middle of nowhere. In this small town, everybody knows your name and your business. They ask me who owns the car in my driveway, if it's one they're not familiar with. I have to get out of town to have a life where no one's watching." The challenges of suburban and urban single pastors may be different. But there, anonymity often doesn't protect them from loneliness, matchmaking, or preconceptions about their availability. In either case, all pastors need friends and activities outside the church to deepen their emotional lives, to add zest to their lives, and to find resources for the long haul.

The Bivocational Pastor

Time with family and for outside activities is a major issue for bivocational pastors, many of whom had steady day jobs when they entered the ministry. Unlike many settled pastors, they have sufficient income, but their congregations, due to size and budget, can afford only part-time pastoral leadership. Still, as the saying goes, time is of the essence, as many bivocational pastors, experiencing themselves as called to ministry in midlife, seek to balance work, ministry, and home life. They have to respond to the needs of an employer or their clients as well as a congregation, not to mention their family.

Andy works as an accountant in a midsized city. Called in midlife to the ministry, he finds tax season a crazy time, in part, because it coincides with Lent, Holy Week, and Easter. In telling his story, Andy reflects, "I felt God's call in college, but I was engaged and needed a steady income for my wife-to-be and, later, for a growing family. I put off God's call till the kids were in college. I had amassed a nest egg and could afford to go to seminary part time. It wasn't easy, going back to school, running a business, and being a husband and parent, but I didn't drop the ball too often. After seminary, I was called to a small suburban congregation, more or less to shut it down. Instead, it grew; while it is still small, nobody's talking about closing the doors. I love the work, but during Holy Week and Lent, which coincide with tax season, I have to make some serious time decisions. . . . I tell my church that I have a business to run and that the best I can do during tax season is prepare good sermons and worship services. Ironically, this has helped them step up to handle most of the pastoral care when I'm busy at work. I am blessed and look forward to retiring in a few years, once the kids are out of college, and devoting myself full time to ministry."

Diane also felt called to ministry in midlife. Like Andy, she attended seminary part time, and because of her husband's work was able to cut her hours in half at work. Still, she struggles with a schedule of marriage, parenting two teens, and working twenty hours as a preschool teacher and another twenty hours at church. "I have to keep good boundaries to be healthy and care for my family. Of course, my husband is supportive. He's taken over the evening meals and helps get the kids off to school in the mornings. I work Sundays and two afternoons a week at church and spend Fridays at home working on sermons. Things happen—emergencies and deaths—and then I have to scramble. The kids are old enough to be home alone, but I don't want to neglect them. I don't have many weddings at this small church, so Saturdays and Sunday afternoons are usually fairly free for family time, with just a little sermon prep. When I work overtime at church, I do my best to take an afternoon off the next week or when it's convenient for the congregation."

Bivocational pastors have to be especially intentional about time and relationships. Good boundaries make good ministries, to paraphrase a poem by Robert Frost, and this is true when we have several equally important responsibilities. Excellence involves the whole person and all her or his responsibilities. It is difficult to maintain excellence in ministry if we neglect our family or day job. As Diane affirms, "I have to say no all the time. Most of the time, it's to myself and my desire to do more ministry than is healthy for me or my family. If I monitor myself well and stay in balance, it's easier to say no to the less important aspects of congregational life. I can't go to everything at church and seldom go to weekend denominational meetings because of my preschool job and family time. But I do participate in the important things."

One last note regarding bivocational ministry: often the salary and benefits for part-time workers are unfair. It is my belief that part-time pastors need to receive, if possible, a prorated percentage of retirement and health care (if it is needed). It goes without saying that they should receive a Social Security offset and a percentage set aside for housing as well. Despite economic challenges, congregations need to aspire to be just in compensation for all their employees: pastors, sextons, janitors, musicians, and administrative assistants.

INTIMACY AND DISTANCE IN MINISTRY

Intimacy is essential to ministry, but so is distance. Pastoral ministry has a built-in solitude; we do our best work when we are "in but not of the congregation." There are unique power dynamics in congregational life and pastoral ministry that pastors need to take seriously. On the one hand, the pastor is an employee of the church. Too much intimacy with congregational lay leaders can make it difficult for the pastor and the laity to be honest with one another and disagree about important issues in healthy ways. On the other hand, the pastor is a spiritual leader, and this intimacy is both a blessing and a challenge. Congregants often transfer deep spiritual and emotional feelings onto their pastors; conversely, pastors may find themselves not only loving but also liking some of their congregants in special, though not unhealthy or inappropriate, ways. Mindfulness is essential for appropriate pastoral relationships. We need to be aware of our own feelings as well as the feelings others have in relationship to us. I recall a situation in a country church where I served as an interim pastor. The church and the study in the parsonage were fairly remote, and virtually no one was on site during the week. When a married congregant seeking guidance about her son's situation confessed wistfully, "It's so great to have someone to talk with. My husband never talks to me. You're such a caring pastor," I knew that any further meetings needed to take place in the local diner! Pastors and congregants may find themselves with close emotional ties; but when a pastor realizes the possibility of "needing" a congregant's companion-ship, even if he or she is acting professionally and ethically, the pastor needs to creatively pull back and seek the counsel of wise colleagues, many of whom have experienced the same interpersonal challenges in ministry.

Many pastors note that especially close relationships within the con-gregation may lead to envy on the part of other congregants or to in-group, out-group dynamics, which compromises a minister's ability to provide healthy spiritual leadership and congregational care. As the spiritual children of monks, mystics, and shamans, pastors need always to claim the mantle of self-awareness. Jesus's willingness to address the temptations of spiritual leadership during his retreat in the wilderness is a model for all healthy pastors. As the saying goes, to have no tempta-tions is the greatest temptation. To be aware of our relational vulner-abilities is a prerequisite for spiritual leadership that nurtures, heals, and transforms.

TIME TO LOVE

When I posted the question "What intentional practices do you find nurture relationships?," one of my former students, a highly skilled Unitarian Universalist minister on the East Coast, joked back at me, "What relationships?" This pastor's comment reflects the difficulties many pastors have claiming time for relationships. Most pastors' sched-ules are at cross-purposes from their families: Partners or spouses and children have weekends off; pastors regularly work weekends. Pastors consistently have evening meetings when families typically are home. And ministerial sabbaticals may provide much needed time for rest and reflection for pastors, but they may cause added duties and stresses for spouses if sabbaticals include time apart from spouses and children. Still, intentionality and mindfulness are central to healthy relationships in ministry. Pastors need to take time to love, whether they are married or single, experienced or new to ministry.

As card-carrying members of the sandwich generation, Kate and I have always appreciated the flexibility of ministry. In the course of the week, we take time to see our son, daughter-in-law, and young grand-children; we also are blessed with the flexibility to provide company and transportation for Kate's ninety-five-year-old mother. Allison, a United Methodist two-point charge pastor concurs, "I put in a fifty-hour week on the average, but I make it a point to visit my mother at her apart-ment twice a week and have my grandchildren over on Fridays and Saturdays." A United Church of Christ pastor, Doug appreciates the flexibility that allows him to drive ninety minutes from his Central Pennsylvania manse to see his grandchildren in Philadelphia most Fri-day afternoons and Saturday mornings. "Unless there is a church meet-ing or obligatory conference event," this single grandparent rejoices, "I take Friday afternoons and Saturdays off to see the boys in Philly and return Saturday evening to put the finishing touches on my sermon and worship service."

Ministry can be stressful on marriages, but it can also be a blessing. A United Methodist pastor, Karla makes time for "planned dates, chil-dren, spouse, and friends. If I just let things happen, then we'd never get together. I am constantly setting times for dinners, hikes, sporting events, and quiet times. Of course, I need to make dates with myself as well to stay centered in ministry." Judy states that she "insists on most Saturdays off—because that is the only day both my husband and I can get off. Yes, occasionally the conference schedules something, but I try to keep it to a minimum. On Saturdays, I focus on our relationship, which sometimes includes sharing in cleaning house. Since my husband is a self-employed IT consultant, we both work at home in the parson-age (the church office is connected to the parsonage), so that helps. I can stop in throughout the day for midmorning or midafternoon coffee or lunch together." It isn't always easy, but pastors can find creative

ways to join ministerial excellence with care for their families and relationships.

Julia sees taking time with her husband and seminary friends as
essential to her emotional and relational well-being. "I am in a very
good Lutheran congregation and like the people, but my emotional
energy is with my friends and family, not the church. I have two consec-
utive days off, usually Friday and Saturday, so at least one of the days
off coincides with my husband's schedule. I also have two clergy friends
with whom I schedule quarterly 'clergy renewal days.' Sometimes we go
out for dinner and a movie, other times we go to a concert or just find a
place for drinks and sharing."

Single pastors need to be just as intentional about relationships as
married pastors. In describing her life, Kelly avers, "I've been single
throughout my ministry. I entered when my children were finishing
high school. I've made it because I've been part of a group of women
pastors who have stayed in touch over the years. We began as pastors in
neighboring towns, now we live across the country; but we visit each
other on holidays and stay in touch by phone, e-mail, and Skype." Kelly
adds that "because I'm in a small-town Episcopal congregation, I
needed to find hobbies that take me outside the church. I took up
painting and learned to play the cello. In both cases, my classes were
half an hour away in the county seat, and that gave me time to add on a
visit to the library or coffee shop or to take myself out to dinner."

As a single workaholic and suburban Congregationalist pastor, Dave
knew he needed an outlet from the church in order to stay healthy in
ministry. He found his outlet in community theater. "I'm usually involved in two plays a year. I get to explore different parts of my personality. I also have the opportunity to meet new people. My congregants
find it humorous when I grow a beard or goatee or sport a crew cut to
be in character for a part. They ask, 'What will he look like next?' It's
been fun and helped me become a better preacher as a result of experience on stage."

A small-town single pastor, Samantha finds companionship in a
group of friends who "get together on Sunday afternoons to quilt and
solve the world's problems. They're outsiders like me, and none of them
are part of the church. We've helped each other get through a lot of
tough times and celebrated a lot of good times."

A thirtysomething pastor, Steve enjoys being with "people who don't know or care that I'm a pastor. I play in a bluegrass band that performs in local coffeehouses and bars. Once in a while, a congregant shows up where I'm playing and is surprised that I'm a musician as well as pastor. I've met a lot of people on the bluegrass circuit; they've introduced me to great food, cold beer, and good companionship." All these pastors, married or single, affirm that their ministries are richer and healthier as a result of a commitment to relationships outside the church. They have an emotional life outside the church that puts an implied boundary on congregational relationships and puts relationships with congregants in a healthy perspective.

HEALTHY PRACTICES FOR HEALTHY PASTORS

Healthy relationships, like physical and spiritual well-being, require a combination of contemplation and action. We need to take stock of our current relational health, explore alternative behaviors, and then reach out to others in healthy and life-transforming ways.

Looking at Your Life

Healthy ministry requires a commitment to self-awareness or mindfulness, which has been at the heart of spiritual practices of Christianity and the other great world religions. Mindfulness involves looking at your life as a prelude to attitudinal and behavioral transformation. In this relational exercise, I invite you to still your spirit prayerfully, whether you're sitting in an easy chair, walking in your neighborhood, or contemplating in your church study. In the quiet of self-examination, undergirded by a sense of God's loving care and affirmation, consider the following:

The balance in your life of work and relationships: are you comfortable with the amount of time you spend with your loved ones, whether family or closest friends?
Are you emotionally available to your loved ones? Are you content with your level of emotional availability? (There is no ideal of

emotional availability; a person's emotional life is shaped by personality type, life experiences, family of origin, and so forth.)

Be both imaginative and honest, putting yourself in the shoes of your loved ones. How would they answer questions of work-relational balance and emotional availability?

What do you need from your loved ones to nurture your well-being personally and professionally? What do they need from you?

What aspects of your current situation would you change to achieve a healthier balance between ministry and relationships and to enhance the quality of your relationships?

What first step can you take today to bring greater joy and health to your relational life?

Take time to pray for transformation, knowing that God is on your side and God will support you through possibilities and energize your quest for relational healing and wholeness. Also important to note is that your spiritual practices may lead you to recognize that change may require the support of trained professionals. Many pastors, including me, have benefited from couples and personal counseling that enables us to heal the past, break old behavior patterns, learn greater acceptance of one another, and explore new behaviors.

Being Present in the Moment

One of my favorite books is Thich Nhat Hanh's *Peace Is Every Step* Similar to Brother Lawrence and the "practice of the presence of God" and Jean Pierre de Caussade and the "sacrament of the present moment," this Buddhist monk invites us to see each moment as holy and to be present to our experiences and the experiences of others wherever we are. According to Thich Nhat Hanh, "In meditation, we stop and look deeply. We stop just to be there, to be with ourselves and the world. . . . Peace and happiness are the fruit of this process. We should master the art of stopping in order to be with our friend and the flower."[1]

The challenge of multitasking and busyness in ministry is that we are never truly with the people who are right beside us. Our bodies are present but our minds are a million miles away. Presence is absolutely necessary in healthy and life-transforming ministry: when an anxious person enters our study or when we visit a congregant in the hospital, we need to breathe deeply, open our spirits, and listen with our hearts as well as our minds. We need to cultivate the ability to drop every other task to be a healing partner with vulnerable people. Sadly, many pastors who seek to be present with their congregants are emotionally absent with their loved ones. Ministers are not alone in this challenge: how often have we seen the caricature of a husband—and I can pick on husbands, since I am thirty-five-year, card-carrying member of the husbands' union—who is reading the newspaper and nodding his head as he repeats "Yes, dear" to everything his wife says, including the possibility that she might jump off a bridge? Or how often have we observed or been guilty of being so engrossed in a television program that the needs of the child who simply wants our attention are overlooked? We are always on holy ground, and the holiest ground is the person right in front of us.

Many of us find it exceedingly difficult to shift gears from ministry to friends and family. When I am teaching people to meditate, I sometimes note that we need to take time to meditate—that is, to be still—before we start to meditate! We need a moment to gather ourselves emotionally—to "consider the lilies," as Jesus says—to be present when we open the door to our homes or meet a friend for coffee or lunch. Tom, who pastors a large midwestern congregation, often chooses to leave his car at church and walk the five blocks home each afternoon. "In the ten minutes of walking home, I turn off the phone, let go of the church for a while, and am emotionally refreshed to be with my family." Theresa, a West Coast pastor, uses her twenty-minute drive home as a "moving monastery." In the quiet of the car, she listens to calming music and breathes deeply, opening and letting go, placing her day in God's hands and trusting that God will be at work while she's off duty. "As a mother of three and the pastor of a busy United Church of Canada congregation, I don't get much time for sitting meditation, but in the car I make it a point to simply be here, just Jesus and me, on the road together, preparing to be Christ's presence in my next stop."

Being present is challenging in a multitasking world. It is, as Thich Nhat Hanh asserts, part of the "miracle of mindfulness" in which you are simply present to the world right where you are. At home, pause, notice, open, and respond to what's happening. Take time to be present for one thing at a time. "Don't worry about the next task," as Jesus counsels. "Consider the child, spouse, or friend in front of you."

When I practice the presence of the holiness of the moment, my greatest challenge is letting go of good ideas I'm writing about or planning for programs I'll be giving. Being a grandparent of two young boys has once again awakened me to wonder of the moment. When the boys come to my home or we're playing at their home, I take a breath, calm my mind, and let go of everything except the baby's bouncing chair, a question about Winnie the Pooh, playing train with Thomas the Train and his friends, adventuring with Dora the Explorer and the Swiper the Fox, and responding to the numerous questions that toddlers have. Frankly, at times, I have to work hard to be fully present with my wife, Kate. We have a long history and many habitual relational patterns, and it's tough to receive each moment with the "beginner's mind," as the Buddhists say. But I am working on rejoicing in this one unrepeatable moment —which is each moment—I am spending with her. It is my desire that she knows that when we are together, she is the most important person in the world and the love of my life, always.

Breathe deeply, let go of many tasks, look deeply at the person with you, and prayerfully celebrate this unrepeatable moment!

Sacred Times

Healthy relationships are grounded in intentionality, openness, and flexible rituals. We need to spend quantity time to experience quality time. One interesting physiological aspect of meditative practices, according to researchers, is that spending fifteen or twenty minutes in quiet meditation calms your body and lowers your blood pressure, even if you have trouble focusing. Quantity time can change the quality of our lives. As Woody Allen notes, "Ninety percent of life is just showing up." Or in the spirit of Beatle John Lennon, life is happening while you're making other plans. Being at home, going to games, sitting while a child does homework, eating out, quietly reading or watching television beside your spouse or partner can open the door to holiness. Showing up is essential, and so is making plans to spend time with friends and loved ones.

I try to walk at least five days a week with my wife. It's often a shorter and more meandering walk than my personal, spiritual power-walks, but in that walk we share what's going on and make plans for the week ahead. Sometimes we just gaze quietly in the same direction. I find that going out to dinner, to a movie, or for a cup of coffee can also be a holy moment that strengthens our relationship. Unfettered by domestic life for a few hours, we discover that new possibilities and plans emerge or we experience the joy of simply being quiet together.

In rituals with loved ones, we need to factor in personality types, and this isn't always easy. I like to spend time at movies, plays, talking over coffee, and walking; my more extroverted wife wants to go out to dance or go out with extroverted friends. She prefers noisy conversation in lively bistros; I would rather sit around a fire alternating between gazing at the flames and entering into conversation. Needless to say, we've had more than a few challenges meeting in the middle socially and recreationally.

As a young parent, I read to my son—just as my dad did when I was a small boy—every morning and every evening. That was our time, and now he does the same with his toddler son. Any place can be a thin place, to use Celtic imagery, where we experience holiness in the passing moments of time. Consider the following questions:

Do you have special times you spend with your spouse or partner?
Do you have rituals with your children and each child in particular? (After all, each child has her or his unique interests and needs your unique responsiveness.)
Do you have special places where you spend time with loved ones— on a regular basis or at certain times during the year (holidays, day trips)?

Friendships beyond the Church

Ministerial wisdom asserts that healthy ministry requires having close relationships outside the church. Eating lunch or even going to a movie with congregants can enhance our lives and ministry. A degree of interpersonal and appropriate intimacy is important in ministerial effectiveness and relationships with congregants. Pastors are not just professionals, we are people too, and our congregants want to get to know us. I have found that just a cup of coffee at a local bistro or café can transform a ministerial relationship in ways that change the life of the church. Differentiation includes intimacy as well as professional distance, and there is great wisdom to the adage "They don't care what you know until they know that you care." Still, we need strong friendships outside church. We need to cultivate meaningful relationships with other adults: with our spouse or partner, colleagues in ministry, friends from seminary, brothers and sisters, and companions on life's way. Though we should not avoid appropriate emotional relationships in ministry, healthy ministry orients us toward positive emotional relationships outside the church. Our needs for intimacy and self-revelation should be addressed among friends, not congregants, in order for us to be most effective in our pastoral leadership roles.

Finding friendships outside the church isn't always easy for single pastors, small-town pastors, or pastors who minister in remote places with few outside activities and where everybody knows your name. This is true for couples as well as single people. Married pastors living in remote places have often commented, "We want to go out with couples for a drink or dinner and a movie, but everyone we know is from the church, and whatever we do in town becomes public knowledge." Pastors need to be especially intentional about cultivating healthy relationships outside the church, even though most adult friendships emerge in school or the workplace.

Some pastors simply leave town for a day or two on a regular basis. A single pastor in an upstate New York village, Shelly rotates on Fridays and Saturdays between going home and getting together with friends in a city two hours away. "I love my church, but when I leave the town limits, I take a deep breath and smile and then I exhale. Now I can play and let my hair down, I can go out with friends and party a bit or go to the mall with my mom and brunch with my parents. I return feeling emotionally replenished and happy with my ministry in my small town." Ian, another single pastor, has joined a number of interest groups to nurture relationships and feed his mind. "I'm part of a book group across town. We drink wine and talk about books. I've met a few good friends through the group. I also like to hike, so I've joined a hiking club that goes on a monthly basis." Terry and Sharon, co-pastors and parents in a small town off the beaten track, don't have the luxury of seeing their parents, who live five hundred miles away, on a regular basis, but they do leave town on day trips and overnights once or twice a month. "When the kids don't have a game or weekend activity, we head out to the woods for a hike, to the mall for shopping and a movie two hours away, or for a Sunday afternoon–Monday getaway when the kids don't have school. We need this for our sanity, because this town can get pretty small. We return in better emotional shape and feeling happier in our work." Terry and Sharon have found a person outside the church who cares for their children when they do an overnight at a bed and breakfast twice a year. On occasion their respective parents, all in their sixties, come up for weekends, enabling them to take a little time away from church and home. Money is always a constraint for them, but they believe their ability to work together requires time away as a couple as well as individual retreats.

It is not good for a pastor to be alone. Healthy ministry doesn't just let things happen; it is grounded in intentionality that makes things happen. Knowing we need friends outside the church for emotional health, intimacy, and joy of life invites us to reach out and explore new behaviors. In the interplay of distance and intimacy, a few friends outside church or special times with children or spouses brings energy and excitement that enable us to share good news over the long haul.

12

LETTING YOUR LIGHT SHINE

This Little Light of Mine

> You are the light of the world. A city built on a hill cannot be hid. No one after lighting a lamp puts it under the bushel basket, but on the lampstand, and it gives light to all in the house. In the same way, let your light shine before others, so that they may see your good works and give glory to your Father in heaven.
>
> —Matthew 5:14–16

JOINING ACTION AND CONTEMPLATION IN MINISTRY

Healthy ministry involves the interplay of contemplation and action, listening to your life and letting your life speak. As a child I heard stories about people of little consequence in the world's eyes who did great things in God's eyes: David and Goliath, Mary the mother of Jesus, the boy with five loaves and two fish. They inspired me to believe that I could make a difference, and they still remind me that small acts of faith performed over a lifetime can transform the world. In my Sunday school class we often sang the Gospel spiritual "This Little Light of Mine." It gave me hope that, small as I was, I could do something important for God.

> This little light of mine,
> I'm going to let it shine.
> Oh, this little light of mine,
> I'm going to let it shine.
> Let it shine, let it shine, let it shine.

> Ev'ry where I go,
> I'm going to let it shine.
> Oh, ev'ry where I go,
> I'm going to let it shine.
> Let it shine, let it shine, let it shine.[1]

Jesus captured the heart of faithful ministry when he proclaimed, "You are the light of the world. . . . Let your light shine before others, so that they may see your good works and give glory to your Father in heaven" (Matt. 5:14, 15). As we conclude this book on clergy self-care, can you affirm Jesus's words by saying, "I am the light of the world"? Can you proclaim, "My light shines to give glory to God and healing and beauty to this good earth and its creatures"? Ministry is about making a difference for God or, as Mother Teresa asserts, doing something beautiful for God. Contemplation and action, self-care and service are intimately connected. Without action, contemplation eventually stagnates and becomes navel gazing; but without contemplation, action leads to burnout and compassion fatigue. We are called to both "picket and pray," as the words written on a bench at Kirkridge Retreat and Study Center proclaim. Our task as spiritual leaders is to let our light shine out in sharing good news through transforming hearts, communities, and social systems. But as another song I learned in childhood asserts, we need oil to keep our lamps burning brightly. We find the energy we need for the long haul through practices of self-care and spiritual formation.

ACTIVE SPIRITUALITY

I have always appreciated the title of Kent Ira Groff's book *Active Spirituality: A Guide for Seekers and Ministers*.[2] Spirituality is active and world changing; it transforms our perspective and inspires us to change the world to reflect God's vision of shalom. Healthy ministry is grounded in an active spirituality in which joining self-care and prayer leads to care for others.

Regardless of the original intent of Jesus's dinnertime dialogue with Mary and Martha, I believe Mary and Martha are archetypes for holistic ministerial excellence. Mary is right in focusing solely on Jesus, but eventually she needs to get up to do the dishes. Martha appropriately prepares supper and decants the wine, but after supper she needs to slow down and enjoy a glass of wine and conversation with Jesus.

I like the Chinese symbolism of yin and yang, receptivity and activity, contemplation and action. Yang includes a dot of yin, and yin holds a dot of yang to remind us that action and contemplation are dynamic and complete each other in a healthy and well-lived life. Healthy ministry integrates yin and yang, contemplation and action, to give glory to God and beauty and justice to the world.

In her quest for healthy ministry, Sheila asserts that "mindfulness is essential to my well-being. As an extrovert, I love to work the crowd and am exhilarated after Sunday mornings. After I've shaken the last hand, I want more . . . I can hardly wait till evening youth group. Left to my own devices, I'd probably work ninety hours a week. But I've ended up in the hospital twice from overwork. What do they say—the spirit is willing, but the flesh is weak! Now I monitor my energy level and intentionally take time away for extroverted spirituality—hiking and singing and going to coffee shops to read." Like Sheila, Dan is also a self-described busy pastor, who is always active in mission projects. He serves on the board of the local shelter and soup kitchen and is on a number of denominational committees on immigration and health care. After years of struggling, he claims to have finally found a balance between social activism and healthy relationships. "For years I was so busy working for justice that I neglected my family. My activism led to alienation with my wife and absence from my children. My kids never said it out loud, but they knew that feeding a homeless person or advocating for an undocumented worker or an evicted family always came first. I wish I'd found a better way to care for my family with the same attention I gave to people in need. It took the threat of divorce to turn me around. Now I spend regular time with my wife. We have a coffee date and a night out each week. And I'm finally getting to know my teenage children. I realized that they needed me as much as any homeless family. I'm still active in the community and denomination, but now I keep an eye on my calendar. In fact, because I'm so obsessed with social justice, I have to block out several times a week as a reminder that family's important, too!"

Michelle has the opposite challenge. Introverted by disposition, this United Methodist pastor is worn out at the thought of working in the church's soup kitchen or going to town hall to advocate policies and

programs that address the needs of people who are homeless and un-
employed. In her words, "I care about justice, but I get tired of people
after a while. I love working on sermons, leading spiritual growth
groups and doing spiritual direction, and preparing for and teaching
classes. I don't have energy for much more sometimes, but I know I
have to push myself to speak up for the poor in our community or to
provide hospitality for the hungry. God calls me in my study and garden, and I feel God's presence most in times of solitude, but I know my
vocation calls me to go out into the community and bring good news."

The Hindu tradition recognizes that several different types of yoga,
or paths to God, are needed, depending on personality type, life experience, and physiology. Perhaps a variety of Christian yoga practices
should be affirmed as a way of providing spiritual and self-care practices
for pastors and their congregants. Ultimately, of course, healthy ministry invites each of us to explore a variety of pathways of spiritual formation and professional emphasis. As I look at my own professional journey, I am grateful that I have integrated teaching, ministry, and administration throughout most of my career. I have been forced to become a
public theologian and mission-oriented pastor. As a result of a lifetime
of extroverted activities that balance my introversion, my professional
life represents a happy medium to such a degree that most people are
surprised to find that I am introverted by nature. I believe my integration of Mary and Martha has been a blessing to myself and others. I
bring my quiet times of prayer and study to my preaching and pastoral
care. My public career has inspired me to be a better scholar and has
been the source of most of my writing, including this book. I still need a
lot of quiet time and need to be mindful of my tendency toward emotional depletion when I have too many external activities. But the dynamic interplay of action and contemplation has enriched my life, deep-
ened my spirituality, and made me a better spouse for my extroverted
wife.

HEALTHY PRACTICES FOR HEALTHY PASTORS

Healthy ministry takes many forms, depending on factors such as age,
personality type, context, and relationships. We need to claim God's
light in our lives and let our light shine. As we conclude our reflections

on healthy ministry and self-care, I invite you to share in the following healthy spiritual practices.

Claiming God's Light in Your Life

John's Gospel proclaims, "⁹The true light, which enlightens everyone, was coming into the world." (1:9). God's light enlightens each of us and shapes our lives, to a greater or lesser degree, depending on our openness. Pastors can affirm for themselves and their congregants, "I am the light of the world" and "You are the light of the world." In this spiritual practice, I invite you to reflect on your spiritual life and leadership by asking the following questions:

Where are you currently experiencing God's guidance and care in your life?

Where have you experienced God's illuminating in the course of your call as a pastor?

What moments of grace did you experience today?

Where are you being invited to share God's loving light in your family, congregation, community, and quest for personal wellbeing?

Experiencing God's Light

Despite preaching about God's grace, many pastors suspect that grace can be found everywhere except in their own lives. Given the realities of ministry and daily life and the impact of our choices over time, we can come to see ourselves as failures as pastors, parents, and partners. Self-examination is essential to Christian life, but the realities of imperfection and the impact of our choices do not exclude us from God's grace. In the order of God's creation, original blessing always precedes human sin. You are loved by God, not in spite of who you are but because you are a child of God, and that is nonnegotiable. In this exercise, you will experience God's loving and healing light in your life as pastor.

Take a moment to sit in a comfortable position and breathe gently, experiencing the influx of energy as you inhale and the reduction of stress as you exhale. After a few minutes, visualize God's loving and healing light entering you with each breath. Visualize God's light filling your whole being from head to toe and healing and cleansing any areas of discomfort and pain, whether physical, emotional, spiritual, or relational. When you experience God's light filling your whole being, imagine yourself being surrounded and enveloped by God's light. You are safe and strong and held in God's loving care. After a few minutes of experiencing yourself wrapped in God's loving light, conclude with a prayer of thanksgiving for God's intimate and personal love for you.

Shining God's Light

This exercise involves both self-examination and imagination as a pathway to joining contemplation and action in life and ministry. Acts of love and reconciliation balanced by times of refreshment are essential to clergy self-care and well-being. Health depends on sharing our gifts and dreams and not hiding them under a bushel basket. In a time of prayerful reflection, consider the following questions:

Where do you experience yourself sharing God's light?
What people inspire you to reach out in love and healing?
What people radiate divine light for you?
Where do you experience yourself being called to share God's love
    and light—personally and professionally? What people inspire
    you to let your light shine in new and creative ways?
Where do you experience yourself being called to share God's love
    as a spiritual leader with the wider community? What visions of
    justice making and earth care are calling you forward in mission
    to the world?

Walking in the Light

As I've noted earlier in the text, I love walking. Whether we are walking, hiking, swimming, jogging, or moving on a stationary bike or elliptical machine, movement enables us to creatively entertain new possibilities in relationships, professional life, and congregational mission. We are not stuck in old ideas and ways of doing things but are moving forward, lured by horizons of hope and adventure. Even people whose ability to physically move is impaired as a result of illness, accident, or incarceration can still move forward in their imaginations.

As you go forth on your own adventures of joining clergy self-care and wellness with active and effective ministry, make a commitment to consciously and intentionally take a few first steps toward personal and professional wholeness. If you have not already begun this process, consider a first step on the pathway toward clergy self-care by responding to these questions as a whole person: body, mind, spirit, and relationships.

What first step can you take for personal refreshment?
What first step can you take in healing and deepening personal and
  professional relationships?
What first step can you take to fulfill your unique vocation as God's
  partner on the pathway to healing the world?

All of us are marching in the light of God, as the South African hymn proclaims, living in the love of God and moving in the power of God. May your journey toward healthy and life-changing ministry be blessed.

I Want To Walk as a Child of the Light

NOTES

1. MINISTRY IN THE TWENTY-FIRST CENTURY

1. Although much of my narrative comes directly from conversations or Internet responses from individuals or groups of pastors, some identifying themselves publicly on Facebook, I have chosen to use pseudonyms and in many cases alter locations for the sake of confidentiality. I will also reflect, mostly in the first person, about my own ministerial encounters, joys, and challenges.

2. Roy Oswald, *Clergy Self-Care* (Herndon, VA: Alban Institute, 1991).

3. For more on current trends in North American spirituality, see Diana Butler Bass, *Christianity after Religion: The End of the Church and the Birth of a New Spiritual Awakening* (New York: HarperOne, 2012); Carol Howard Merritt, *Tribal Church: Ministering to the Missing Generation* (Herndon, VA: Alban Institute, 2007); Lillian Daniel, *When Spiritual But Not Religious Is Not Good Enough: Seeing God in Surprising Places, Even the Church* (Nashville: Jericho Books, 2013); Bruce Epperly, *Emerging Process: Adventurous Theology for a Missional Church* (Cleveland, TN: Parson's Porch Books, 2011).

2. DO YOU WANT TO BE MADE WELL?

1. Barbara Brown Taylor, *Leaving Church: A Memoir of Faith* (New York: HarperSanFrancisco, 2007), 5.

2. Ibid., 98.

3. Ibid., 75.

3. LIVING BY ABUNDANCE IN A TIME OF SCARCITY

1. "A New Creed," The United Church of Canada website, Beliefs, http://www.united-church.ca/beliefs/creed.

2. For more on Philippians, see Bruce Epperly, *Philippians: A Participatory Study Guide* (Gonzales, FL: Energion, 2011).

5. GLORIFY GOD IN YOUR BODY

1. For a more thorough discussion of the importance of the body and healing in Jesus's ministry, see Morton Kelsey, *Healing and Christianity* (Minneapolis: Fortress Press, 1995); and Bruce Epperly, *God's Touch: Faith, Wholeness, and the Healing Miracles of Jesus* (Louisville, KY: Westminster/John Knox, 2001); *Healing Worship: Purpose and Practice* (Cleveland: Pilgrim Press, 2006); and *Healing Marks: Healing and Spirituality in Mark's Gospel* (Gonzales, FL: Energion, 2013).

2. Jana Childers, ed., *Birthing a Sermon: Women Preachers on the Creative Process* (St. Louis: Chalice Press, 2001), 5.

3. Dan Millman, *The Way of the Peaceful Warrior* (Novato, CA: H. J. Kramer, 2006).

4. Suzanne Schmidt and Krista Kurth, *Running on Plenty at Work: Renewal Strategies for Individuals* (Washington, DC: Renewal Resources, 2003).

5. For more on Reiki healing touch, see Bruce Epperly and Katherine Epperly, *Reiki Healing Touch and the Way of Jesus* (Kelowna, British Columbia: Northstone Press, 2005).

6. Elizabeth O'Connor, *Journey Inward, Journey Outward* (New York: Harper Collins, 1975).

7. Susan Cain, *Quiet: The Power of Introverts in a World That Can't Stop Talking* (New York: Broadway, 2013).

8. For more on the importance of personality types in shaping our lives and ministries, see Bruce and Katherine Epperly, *Feed the Fire: Avoiding Clergy Burnout* (Cleveland: Pilgrim Press, 2008).

6. LOVING GOD WITH YOUR WHOLE MIND

1. Shirley D. McCune and Edgar W. Mills, "Continuing Education for Ministers: A Pilot Evaluation of Three Programs," ERIC, ED.gov Institute of Education Sciences website, http://www.eric.ed.gov/ERICWebPortal/search/

detailmini.jsp?_nfpb=true&_&ERICExtSearch_SearchValue_0=ED024870&
ERICExtSearch_SearchType_0=no&accno=ED024870.

7. HAVING THE TIME OF YOUR LIFE: MAKING FRIENDS WITH TIME IN MINISTRY

1. Henry van Dyke, "For Katrina's Sundial," *The Poems of Henry van Dyke* (Rockville, MD: Wildside Press, 2008), 240.

2. To hear Carrie Newcomer sing this, consult http://www.youtube.com/watch?v=2qZyoRiBteI. "Holy as a Day is Spent" from A Gathering of Spirits.

8. IGNITING YOUR SPIRIT

1. Bruce and Katherine Epperly, *Reiki Healing Touch and the Way of Jesus* (Kelowna, British Columbia: Northstone Press, 2005).

2. For more on ministerial spirituality and personality type, Bruce and Katherine Epperly, *Feed the Fire: Avoiding Clergy Burnout* (Cleveland: Pilgrim Press, 2008), 139–57.

9. SETTING YOUR SPIRITUAL GPS

1. Parker Palmer, "The Clearness Committee: A Communal Approach to Discernment," The Center for Courage and Renewal, http://www.couragerenewal.org/parker/writings/clearness-committee.

2. For more on visionary leadership, see Bruce G. Epperly and Katherine Gould Epperly, *Tending to the Holy: The Practice of the Presence of God in Ministry* (Herndon, VA: Alban Institute, 2009), 119–58.

3. Dag Hammarskjold, *Markings* (New York: Vintage, 1989), 89.

4. Chris Hobgood, *Welcoming Resistance* (Herndon, VA: Alban Institute, 2002).

10. EMBRACING GRIEF

1. I am pleased that Georgetown University Law Center now has an ongoing program "Lawyers in Balance" to respond to the stresses of law school and

the legal profession. For more information on this program, visit the Georgetown Law website and the web page "Lawyers in Balance": http://www.law. georgetown.edu/campus-life/health-wellness/lawyers-in-balance/index.cfm.

2. "Great Is Thy Faithfulness," text by Thomas Chisholm.

3. William Dean and Larry Axel, *The Size of God: The Theology of Bernard Loomer in Context* (Macon, GA: Mercer University Press, 1987), 30. For further discussion of Loomer's understanding of stature, see pages 30–51.

4. "Blest Be the Tie That Binds," text by John Fawcett.

5. Henri Nouwen, *The Inner Voice of Love* (New York: Doubleday, 1996), 7.

11. HEALTHY RELATIONSHIPS

1. Thich Nhat Hanh, *Peace Is Every Step* (New York: Bantam Books, 1991), 39.

12. LETTING YOUR LIGHT SHINE

1. "This Little Light of Mine," text by Henry Dixon Loes.

2. Kent Ira Groff, *Active Spirituality: A Guide for Seekers and Ministers* (Herndon, VA: Alban Institute, 1993).

ABOUT THE AUTHOR

Bruce Epperly is a practical theologian, pastor, spiritual guide, and author. He served as director of continuing education and professor of practical theology at Lancaster Theological Seminary. An ordained minister in the Christian Church (Disciples of Christ) with standing in the United Church of Christ, he has written thirty books, including *Starting with Spirit: Nurturing Your Call to Pastoral Ministry* and *Tending to the Holy: The Practice of the Presence of God in Ministry*. He and his wife Kate live on Cape Cod, where he is pastor of South Congregational Church in Centerville, Massachusetts.